Praise for A. C. G

'We are mystified, alarmed, even frightened by the cascade of events that beset our world. A. C. Grayling not only clarifies the way in which these events are challenging the workings of democracy – amid the rise in populism in response – but comes up with solutions.'

Jon Snow

'A. C. Grayling applies his great intellectual prowess to the most pressing issue of our times – the subversion of modern democracies by dark money, corporate power, Big Data, social media and fractured political party systems. Utterly brilliant. Urgently needed. A book for NOW.'

Helena Kennedy, KC

'A must read for anyone with questions, worries and fears about pollution, poverty, protectionism, populism, weapons proliferation, and where our world is headed.'

Gordon Brown

'A. C. Grayling tackles the questions science can't answer ... a breathtaking book ... Scholarly, lucid and accessible without being patronising or diluting.'

Telegraph

'Grayling writes with clarity, elegance and the occasional aphoristic twist ... straight alpha material.'

Independent

Also by A. C. Grayling

The History of Philosophy
The Future of Moral Values
What Is Good?
Among the Dead Cities
Against All Gods
Towards the Light
The Choice of Hercules
Ideas that Matter
To Set Prometheus Free
Liberty in the Age of Terror
The Good Book
The God Argument
The Age of Genius
Democracy and Its Crisis
The Good State
The Frontiers of Knowledge
For the Good of the World
Philosophy and Life
Who Owns the Moon?

Discriminations

Achieving Peace
in the Culture Wars

A. C. GRAYLING

ONEWORLD

A Oneworld Book

First published by Oneworld Publications Ltd in 2025

Copyright © A. C. Grayling, 2025

The moral right of A. C. Grayling to be identified as the Author of this work has been asserted by him in accordance with the Copyright, Designs, and Patents Act 1988

All rights reserved
Copyright under Berne Convention
A CIP record for this title is available from the British Library

ISBN 978-0-86154-996-2
eISBN 978-0-86154-997-9

Typeset by Geethik Technologies
Printed and bound in Great Britain by Clays Ltd, Elcograf S.p.A.

No part of this publication may be reproduced, stored in a retrieval system, or transmitted, in any form or by any means, electronic, mechanical, photocopying, recording or otherwise, without the prior permission of the publishers.

The authorised representative in the EEA is eucomply OÜ,
Pärnu mnt 139b–14, 11317 Tallinn, Estonia
(email: hello@eucompliancepartner.com / phone: +33757690241)

Oneworld Publications Ltd.
10 Bloomsbury Street
London WC1B 3SR
England

Stay up to date with the latest books,
special offers, and exclusive content from
Oneworld with our newsletter

Sign up on our website
oneworld-publications.com

MIX
Paper | Supporting
responsible forestry
FSC® C018072

CONTENTS

Acknowledgements ix
Preface xi

Introduction 1

1 Divide and Cancel 11
2 Ideas and Orientations 36
3 Othering, Excluding and Cancelling *Groups* 76
4 Othering, Excluding and Cancelling *Individuals* 106
5 Right(s) and Wrong(s) 130
6 Concerns and Comparisons 164
7 The Bottom Line 189
8 Roads to *Pax Humana* 211

DISCRIMINATIONS

Notes 226
Index 257

For Georgina, Madeleine and Eva,
and in memory of Johnny Penza

ACKNOWLEDGEMENTS

Discussions with too many to mention over the years have been valuable to development of the thoughts here, but my particular thanks go to Sam Carter, Ron Witton, Craig Stanbury, Eloise O'Reilly, Hannah Haseloff, John Grayling and Sarah Wilson; and to Miranda Fricker for insightful comments on chapter 6.

PREFACE

'Wokism' and 'cancel culture' became terms of war – culture war – in the second decade of the twenty-first century. The war itself had already been long in progress, the issues at stake of universal significance; only the terms were new.[1] The place of 'wokism' as an episode in an extended struggle will doubtless be explained better by future historians than by contemporary commentators, but because the issues involved matter so much and are so divisive, standing aside is not an option. For what is at stake for its proponents is an ugly thing: *discrimination* – in the forms of racism, sexism and hostility to life choices that do not conform to a putative norm – and the great harm discrimination does.

The current version of the woke battle consists in claim and counterclaim in so many books, podcasts, YouTube discussions, TV debates, demonstrations and outcries, that the smoke, and the heat generating it, almost wholly obscure the truths at stake, and make it hard to see a way to resolutions. But because tumultuous times are also times of opportunity to address problems, it is worth making efforts in that direction. The effort here is to bring a philosophical perspective to the debate, for it turns on what philosophy fundamentally addresses: ideas and viewpoints, and how to discriminate – here the term has a positive meaning – between what is right and wrong in them. Philosophy seeks to dig deeper and see further, but that does not mean it is neutral; there are crucial rights and serious wrongs at issue in the 'woke wars', and clear recognition of them is indispensable.

It is optimistic to think that an attempt at analysis will be accepted as such by the combatants, both sides viewing someone who tries to engage with the issues as, suspiciously, a covert agent of the opposing side. The suspicion will be heightened because it is impossible for anyone not superhuman to be without sympathies – intellectual as well as emotional – tending to one of the sides. I will therefore disclose straight away that my own sympathies, both intellectually and emotionally, lie in the woke direction – more accurately, with the concerns that prompt wokism – recognising that 'woke' is now a pejorative term in the lexicon of those who, opposing its more vigorous manifestations, label all advocacy for its causes. But I also see the force not just of objections to how some activist endeavours are conducted, but to expressions of concern that the anti-woke side have about such issues as 'mob justice' and free speech denial. Given that these can harm the woke causes themselves, finding a way to promote them without yielding the moral high ground to anti-woke proponents is, very obviously, desirable.

PREFACE

To salvage what is genuinely good out of the battle, even indeed to make its outcome an advance, constructive rather than destructive, and not merely acceptable but even satisfying to all, would be wonderful. That an aim is idealistic is no reason for not attempting it; the realistic part of idealism is that one gets closer to achieving its goal than by not trying at all. That attempt is the aim of this book.

INTRODUCTION

Two broad themes make up history: humanity's progresses and humanity's regresses. In both cases it is ideas – in the form of beliefs, ideologies, hopes and fears – that motivate what happens. Humans are a social species, evolved to exist in communities in which co-operation and reciprocation are the bonds; but the same impulse to community is also an impulse to tribalism, the grouping that fosters and protects an Us against an It – the world's challenges – and a Them; more specifically, Others: other people, other tribes.

These simple generalisations are uncontroversial, but of course they mask much complexity. For one important example: the bigger a tribe, the more sub-tribes and mini-tribes exist within it, their boundaries – however ill-defined and permeable – themselves sites of otherings, competition and conflict. For another example: like other social species, human groups tend to organise themselves hierarchically, a feature that grows more marked as tribes grow larger and more internally complex. The hierarchies can be formal or informal, but they are underwritten by a feature of human nature which seems permanent: the propensity of people to look for leaders, and to cluster under them. The leaders offer ideas, or an Idea, and often with it thereby an Identity – and the identity is the source of the othering that, in providing a bond for some, necessarily 'others' Others.

These latter are generalisations too, but they capture much that has to be considered when wondering how progress is to be enhanced and regress avoided in our still-evolving, imperfect, clever but insufficiently wise species. 'Clever but insufficiently wise': it was Theodor Adorno who said, contemplating humanity's ingenuity in developing the spear into the guided missile, 'We have grown cleverer but not wiser', for had we grown wiser we would not have misapplied our cleverness to ever more murderous weapons.

The big challenge therefore is how to use our cleverness wisely. Among other things, this involves recognising that almost every advance made by humanity has cast a shadow. Our remote ancestors acquired language; with it we can discuss, share, communicate, write poetry, sing songs of love; and with it we can hurl insults, tell lies, abuse and cheat. On looking around, we see the products of co-operation and planning: schools, hospitals, electricity and water supplies. The same survey can also show the rubble of bombing, corpses in the street, starving children, marching columns of troops, straggling files of refugees. Love and hatred, laughter and tears: we know which side we should be on, yet as we close in on the pixels of human experience we find too little of the love and laughter, and too many tears.

INTRODUCTION

Given the facts of human nature, an alloy that brings almost all of both good and bad into human experience, it is utopian to think that some earthly version of heaven will one day be realised. And if it were, its very perfection would, paradoxically, be a negative thing; such a bland dispensation would be, or would soon become, as insupportable as the misery that humanity so often inflicts on itself. Grit is needed between the millstones that produce our poetry, or at least much of it; the poignancy, the beauty, of some of the deepest expressions of human creativity emerge from suffering. But we do not have to manufacture suffering so that there can be poetry. There is enough of it already in the nature of things. We need only realise, and accept, that simply existing already contains plenty of occasions for it. Take the most obvious examples: to fall in love is to make a contract with sorrow, because one of the lovers will die first or fall out of love and leave; to strive to attain a goal is to court failure; to hope is to face the possibility of disappointment. Merely to be alive is to experience illness and death some day. There is enough to contend with that will squeeze the best of our poetry and kindness out of us, without making matters worse by adding jealousy and greed, antipathies and grudges.

There is, on the other hand, enough good in existence to prompt poetry and kindness, and we indeed find or create more than sufficient amounts of it to make existence worthwhile, or better. Yet we still busy ourselves with antipathies, and when we fail to manage them we take the last resort – a terrible mark of failure – of manufacturing bombs and dropping them. And then, alas, when the consequences of dropping them appear, we too often turn our eyes away, seeking to avoid the overwhelming evidence of harm that we and our systems, our behaviour and our choices, have brought about.

Above all, we do too little – though a few, too few, strive mightily otherwise – to address the causes of antipathies which have this result. How are we to put things right? Where do we start?

Well: we start at home, of course – with ourselves, in our societies; and what we start with is our thinking. One could be almost anywhere at any time in history to see the same truths. Starting at home for us is a version, another example, of what has always needed to be addressed. In the pages to follow the discussion could, with a few changes of terminology, apply variously in the ancient worlds of Sumer, Greece and Rome, in Tang Dynasty China, in Renaissance Italy, in Mughal India, in Victorian Britain, in today's United States. This is the effect of persisting traits in human nature, and the fact that apparently diverse structures of society in all those times and places reflect fundamentals in attempts at social organisation – together with the disorganisations and injustices they create.

Competition can be as fruitful as co-operation in driving progress. Conflict, a very different matter, is less fruitful in this way; it too often causes regress. Conflict arises when attempts at progress meet resistance, as they often do, and aspects even of well-intentioned endeavour can turn toxic out of frustration and anger. This is an increasing feature of the

INTRODUCTION

struggles in contemporary societies where some degree of progress has been made in the direction of human rights and civil liberties – the societies loosely grouped as 'Western' – but it is not yet progress enough, and therefore it is still being fought for. Indeed, such progress as has so far been made is threatened not just by those whom it inconveniences, but even by itself when it allows its frustrations to become self-defeating.

Starting at home means starting with these strands of division in our own day. Movements that started in the past – the anti-slavery movement beginning in the eighteenth century, the endeavour to secure employment rights and decent conditions for wage-earners in the nineteenth century, the increased social and economic emancipation of women that began to have traction in the twentieth century – have developed today into further endeavours towards global inclusivity and greater social justice, combatting discrimination and socio-political structures of exclusion which advantage certain groups over others. Some of the more activist champions of this endeavour, frustrated by the too-common phenomenon of a step back for every two steps forward, act in ways that are said, even by those who agree with them but adopt less confrontational methods, to risk undermining the cause by their action – for example, free speech denial and undiscriminating 'cancellings'. This is significant, because the conflicts and regresses in human history are all about precisely this: a dialectic of oppressions, of waking up to being oppressed, attempts to suppress the oppressors in turn, the mutual effort to silence or extirpate each other – to

5

silence or extirpate each Other – with the pain and difficulty thus caused.

Context is all. The following pages aim to provide it for today's continuing struggle for those aims – inclusivity and greater justice – which have yet to be attained.[1]

***

The anchorage of my approach in what follows is to commit without reservation to the principle that the concept of *human rights* is fundamental to solving the problems at issue.[2] There is much to be said about the history, nature and justification of this concept, and some of it is indeed said in these pages. But here at the outset the following two points must be made.

First, the contemporary discourse of human rights was shaped in direct reaction to a monstrous example of atrocity. Drafters of the newly established United Nations 'Universal Declaration of Human Rights', adopted in 1948, had before their eyes the immense suffering and destruction that took place in the 1930s and 1940s across the world from China and Japan to south Asia to much of Europe. They saw the rubble of cities, the corpses of men, women and children, the subjection of millions to inhuman treatment extending to genocide, the negation of every normal expectation that one individual might have of another. Humanity's experience of suffering, so graphically manifest in that period, is by itself an absolute and unequivocal justification of the rights set out in the Declaration.

INTRODUCTION

Atrocities and inhumanities were not novelties in the twentieth century, except in scale; human history had already been scarred by many precedents. And those precedents had already suggested what kinds of principles are needed to combat their occurrence. For centuries, in fact millennia, ideas at least implicitly embodying some of these principles have been put forward. Hints in the Code of Hammurabi in the eighteenth century BCE, and much more explicitly in the 'Axial Age' of the seventh to fourth centuries BCE in India, China, Greece and the Near East, including the Stoics' idea of the universal siblinghood of humankind and the development of law in Roman jurisprudence, contain implicit recognition of much of what is right for human beings in their lives and their relationships both with others and with society.

All this was certainly very imperfect; the past tolerated slavery, the subjection of women, harsh punishments for activities regarded at this or that place or time as sins, crimes and heresies. But the seeds were there, and in the movements mentioned above against slavery and on behalf of workers and women, beginning in the Enlightenment, the seeds began to sprout. What happened in the devastations in human experience that occurred in the 1930s and 1940s brought to a head the need to state loudly, clearly and explicitly what has to be accorded to every human being, just *qua* human being, as inalienable and ultimate in the way of rights. The rights identified are staringly obvious, and such qualifications of them that have to be tolerated in particular circumstances require a justification that is both overwhelming and restricted.

DISCRIMINATIONS

The existence of the Declaration, and the adoption of subsequent human rights instruments derived from it, have not stopped atrocities and inhumanities. But they provide a benchmark and a tool for resisting violations of the principles they assert. They bring into clear focus what we can demand, and what we must do in response to the demands when others make them. They promise a remedy, and if they were to be fully and universally applied the world would be a greatly better place.

Both sides in today's 'woke wars' can and do make appeal, explicitly or implicitly, to these rights. Both sides charge the other with explicit or implicit, actual or threatened, violations of them. Both sides are right in some of these charges. Are there conflicts between the rights invoked? Do any of them have greater weight than others? How are applications of the rights to be made in the light of circumstances in which violation of them, or even just compromised access to their exercise, occurs? These questions are at the heart of trying to bring peace to the 'woke wars', as the latest iteration of the struggle to get these crucial rights implemented. And a major part of that is to get the contending parties to recognise that they are all in fact justified in claiming that rights are being denied or threatened, different rights mattering so much to different parties that they fail to see what is at stake in others' concern for the rights they wish to see implemented or protected. The fallacy at work in the quarrel is that exercise of rights is a zero-sum game: 'if you exercise that right, I can't exercise this one'. This might not appear fallacious given that it sometimes seems that one person's or group's exercise of rights results in denial of a right or rights to others, but the principle that no exercise of a right can deny the exercise of the same right by another, and no exercise of any right can deny the *fundamental* rights of others, rules out conflicts of rights and alerts one to the likelihood that what is actually happening is that the conflict is between the *interests* of one party and the *rights* of the other party. This important point is explored more fully later.[3]

Second, an unrecognised fact about the concept of human rights is that it constitutes an ethics which transcends outlooks constituted by traditions that are socially and historically parochial.[4] Proponents of certain outlooks seek to deny the universality of human rights; in e.g. the People's Republic of China, society's claims are taken to outweigh the claims of individuals; in Islam, rights are to be understood as subject to Shariah law, which qualifies or denies the applicability of some of the Declaration's principles.[5] But the basis for identifying factors that conduce to a decent human existence, applicable to human beings just *qua* human beings, is established by the manifest results of their absence. No matter whether you live in China or France, under Shariah law or the Basic Law of Germany, you are denied what conduces to a decent human existence if you are tortured and denied privacy; if you are unable to hold or express opinions; if you lack access to information relevant to your needs or are prevented from congregating with others, among other rights. And that is the essential point.

For this reason I take the concept of human rights as anchorage in the stormy seas of cultural and political debates. A moment's honest pause on all sides to consider them would

DISCRIMINATIONS

do much towards bringing peace, and with it progress. And crucially, the principle to be observed throughout is, as the great international jurist Sir Hersch Lauterpacht put it in 1943 in the midst of the atrocities of the Second World War, 'The individual human being ... is the ultimate unit of all law'.

1

DIVIDE AND CANCEL

At the time these words were written the United States, the United Kingdom and other polities usually grouped as 'Western' were witnessing an often bad-tempered debate – the 'woke wars' – in which, among other things, the topic of 'cancel culture' took a significant part. This was a development from a preceding half-century and more of increasing activity in movements aimed at promoting greater inclusivity and fairness in society, combatting discrimination, particularly in its forms of sexism, racism, hostility to alternative sexualities and life choices, and addressing the social exclusion faced by those who struggle to navigate the complexities of modern life, as well as the structural obstacles encountered by those who are physically and mentally disabled. The parallel development of greater economic inequalities, marked notably by the dramatically widening global gap between rich and poor, added urgency to the debates. After the Second World War, civil rights movements and second wave feminism gathered momentum, the 1960s and 1970s a significant moment for them. Starting in the late 1980s the concept of 'political correctness' captured what the inclusivity and anti-discrimination movements saw as an essential target: not just behaviour but also language that embodies exclusion, marginalisation, even insult, against groups 'othered' by dominant sections of society. The phrase was, in fact, an ironic borrowing by opponents of the social justice movements, invoking the 'what you say is true but not politically correct' reference to enforced control of thought and speech among those living under (or who, from other countries, looked to) Soviet communism in the period between the two world wars, and therefore chiefly used by those who thought the inclusivity movements were going too far. It was thus a pejorative term, abbreviated to 'PC', a label scornfully intended to denote excess in the relevant respects.[1] But as a term that marks an era, it reminds one that following the 1960s rise of civil rights and feminist activism, continuing in alternating periods of greater and lesser salience since, its use is one among a number of marks of the new era of focus upon *rights*.

In the first decades of the twenty-first century the continuation of efforts to advance social and economic justice, to which were added anxious efforts to prevent or minimise further harm to the natural environment and the planet's climate, took a turn potentiated by the coming of social media. This enabled all with access to it to publish their views if they wished, mounting attacks on, or defences of, institutions and individuals, and thereby generating yet greater movements of opinion. While some of what social media enables consists in interesting and intelligent commentary, great swathes of its content are merely invective, untruth and hatred. Behind the veil of anonymity and with the supreme facility and immediacy of pressing a few buttons, anyone can say what they like about anything. The result has been a flood of sewage into the public conversation in which it is not always easy to spot the good things.

In the rhetorical dimension of the current moment in these movements, the phrase that stands out to anyone interested in historical context is 'cancel culture', because the vast litany of conflicts and regressions in history are exactly described by it; history is over-full of efforts by one group to 'cancel' another in all the ways of othering, excluding, suppressing, silencing, even literally exterminating. In its contemporary usage the phrase recapitulates the same sentiment; it denotes not just the claim that an individual or group has suffered *de facto* cancellation by the violation of their rights, but a reactive determination to cancel the cancellers themselves. This can and often does take the form of action to deprive opponents not only of a platform to state their *views*, but to deprive the *persons* and groups themselves of a presence – at least in the debate; at the extreme, to get rid of their presence altogether. In the case of individuals who are 'cancelled' this can mean the loss of employment and position, social marginalisation and complete silencing – an outcome welcomed by the cancellers, who take themselves to have removed a poison thorn from the body of society; to have erased sin, or punished crime, or combatted heresy, as they see sins, crimes and heresies from their perspective. Their justification is that those they cancelled are themselves cancellers – of the rights, opportunities, dignity of whole swathes of others, perpetuating historical injustices into the present.

Many of those subjected to cancel activism indeed merit being challenged when what they do causes any of the many harms arising from discrimination. The aim of making society, including its economic structures, more inclusive and fair is a noble one – saying this declares a position in the debate – which can alternatively be put by saying that the full application of human rights as civil liberties is a paramount goal. Making them so requires reform of those aspects of society that introduce distortions which prevent many, even indeed majorities, from accessing opportunities and social goods enjoyed by those whom the distortions favour. In the first decades of the twenty-first century a large jump in economic inequality prompted an equally large intensification of the history-long struggle to combat those distortions, social media providing new tools for the task. As those campaigning for greater social justice made gains, they galvanised reaction from conservatives wishing to protect a status quo that serves them well; hence the bitter divides in the form of 'culture war' and political rivalries. The stand-out example is the United States, where politics of both the Washington and cultural kinds approaches the condition of civil war.

Some will perceive an irony, others a rightfulness, in cancellation as a weapon of 'woke' activism, given that it is a product of efforts to raise the visibility and amplify the voices of people who have suffered historical cancellation of particularly oppressive kinds, all the way from marginalisation, prejudice, persecution by morality and law, to the horrors of slavery and the extreme of mass murder. Those who see irony ask: cannot the champions of those who still experience the effects of historical cancellation see that they are combatting forms of oppression by the same form of oppression, donning the robes of their enemy? Those who see rightfulness ask: what should, or can, campaigners do instead in order to achieve greater social and economic justice for women, people of colour, people of different or no religion, and people of sexualities and life choices different from traditional norms, who have been discriminated against historically, and still are?

There is a different irony, though; that the beneficiaries of discriminatory socio-political arrangements have been handed a weapon by the champions of the historically oppressed, because in making themselves oppressors in turn, these champions – or some of them; but all the champions come to be painted in the colours of the more radical among them – thus supply their opponents with rope to hang them. This is particularly so in connection with *freedom of expression*, now claimed as a weapon by the political Right, which once reserved this freedom exclusively for itself but now positions itself as its doughtiest general champion.

By its nature 'cancelling', by whomever done, is a sharp form of censorship and marginalisation, the shutting down of voices, the silencing of debate, ostracism – precisely what the victims of historical cancellation themselves suffered. In taking the instruments of these oppressions into their own hands and using them as they were used in the past, the more radical champions of justice argue that they are justified; they are fighting fire with fire. Are they right, even as they empower their opponents in this way? Again the crucial question presses: what should, or can, they do instead?

The nature of 'cancel culture' can be illuminated by considering instances of its application before the phrase itself became current. For example: Oscar Wilde was a victim of late Victorian cancel culture. He was bisexual, and extrovert; he poked the bear of public opinion with a sharp stick; his attitudes and practices were abominated by those who took themselves to hold the right beliefs and to live in the right way. He was therefore thoroughly, decisively and completely cancelled ('completely' short of actual hanging), by being imprisoned and then banished, dying in exile shortly afterwards. Those who drove him out of society were appalled by him, disgusted by his behaviour, not just offended to the core by him but determined that his toxic example should not be allowed to damage society itself. He had committed what, in their eyes, were all three of sins, crimes and heresies – sin in the eyes of morality, crime in the eyes of the law, heresy against social norms and expectations. Leaving aside questions of right and wrong – about which, much more later – the cancellation of an individual today, driven from a job and unemployable elsewhere because it is not just her or him but whoever employs or allies themselves with her or him who comes under proscription, is no different in its effects.

'Short of actual hanging'; alas, cancelling in history was at its extremer end exactly that – physical torture, hanging, burning at the stake, mass slaughter, the Holocaust of European Jewry, the Holodomor of Ukrainian kulaks, the attempted genocides of Armenians by Turks and of Tutsi by Hutu: are all cancellings. History groans under the terrible weight of cancelling. It is argued – not just by its political opponents but by those on the same side who seek to do things differently – that to normalise even its less drastic forms is not merely retrogressive, but dangerous. Against the cancel culture of the past, a long and arduous battle was fought to liberate voices and thus the people themselves in whose throats those voices were stifled.[2] A measure of victory was – has been – achieved in parts of the world where enlightenment, or Enlightenment, has occurred; only a minority of humankind has so far benefitted in this respect, yet it is in that very minority where the human right, the civil liberty, has been gained to speak out, oppose, campaign, argue and protest, that cancel culture flourishes anew, precisely because it is enabled by the freedoms thus gained. Irony here piles atop irony. The freedom enjoyed by some to deny freedom to others is not what the long struggles for freedom aimed to achieve, but instead to end: by providing freedom of expression to everyone.

'To everyone'? Immediately it will be asked: what to do about horrible, dangerous views? What about Fascists, Stalinists, racists, sexists, homophobes? Should they be free to continue advocacy for their outlook and to seek to put it into practice? What about the people who suffer, either actively in the present or in consequence of historical injustices whose effects linger in palpable ways from the past? One would wish to extirpate horrible and dangerous *views*, indeed one should strive to do so, because of their ugly effects on individuals and groups. What of the *people* who espouse and advocate such views, who put them into effect? One would wish to defeat them, remove them from the path of progress to greater justice in the world. How is one to do either of these things – so a cancel activist will demand – other than by cancelling them?

The standard response – that the way to do it is by education, by having better arguments than the bad people have, by exposing poisonous views and those who purvey them to challenge and ridicule – is met with scepticism by cancel activists on the grounds that these measures are too soft, wishy-washy, ineffective, take too long, do not meet the urgent case of those suffering oppression right now. There is force in this scepticism. An all-too-common observation is that any degree of tolerance leaves a gap for the intolerant to wriggle through. Accordingly the implicit thought is that, as fire is to be combatted by fire, intolerance is not to be tolerated. Activists could even go so far as to claim that there is something literally Christian about this; 'if thy right hand offend thee, cut it off and cast it from thee', for – so the same passage (Matthew, chapter 5, for those interested) goes emphatically on – unless your righteousness exceeds that of others, you will not gain the Kingdom of Heaven. And that is where the social justice movements are headed. And – speaking figuratively of course – rightly headed, providing the aim is not to replace one set of injustices with another.

But the question, almost literally, burns: is this the right way? If not, can the 'standard response' as just described ever be enough? In particular, on what grounds can the righteousness of the righteous in this arena be so justified as to license cancelling? There are rights and wrongs in these important, indeed essential, debates; there are sincere and concerned participants on both sides; how are we to make a secure case for claiming what is right and what is wrong?

There are two major points to be addressed in seeking to answer these questions, and this book seeks to do so.

The first point is to understand thoroughly the nature of cancelling, to see what it has been, what it is and what it too easily can become. In discussing this point, one learns what the issues involved turned on, what arguments and endeavours were used on both sides, and what the fight against oppression achieved – among the achievements being the very freedom that today's cancel activists themselves rely upon to make their case.

The second point – and it is an even greater one – is the question of rights and wrongs itself. This is the nub of the issue. To illustrate what is at stake in this point, a particularly acute example offers itself, one that will perhaps come as a surprise at first: the cancellation in extreme form of Osama bin Laden.

Bin Laden was responsible for acts of terrorism of an horrific kind, the most egregious being the 9/11 atrocity. It was an atrocity for which its instigators and perpetrators merit both condign punishment and the deepest contempt.[3] Bin Laden himself was eventually punished by US Navy SEALs Team Six in their assault on 2 May 2011 on the compound in Abbottabad, Pakistan, where he was hiding. He was killed, and his body is said to have been taken to a US ship in the Persian Gulf and dropped into its waters.[4]

The practical justification for killing bin Laden and disposing of his remains in an anonymous location was that, if he had been captured and taken to Guantanamo Bay, he would have remained a focus of attention and loyalty by followers, more of a martyr to them than he is as a corpse. To effect such decisive closure on the case of bin Laden was seen not only as justified punishment for his crimes but as a swiftly practical way of avoiding further complications. The judgement to this effect was arrived at deliberatively by the President of the United States and his advisers, and it is understandable in the geopolitical circumstances of the 'war on terror' in which, by the terms of that rhetoric, bin Laden could be construed as an enemy combatant.

Here is the 'but': but this punishment of bin Laden was carried out by an advanced Western state claiming to situate itself on principles of the rule of law and human rights. The rule of law entails that a due process is to be followed that involves the right of an accused to hear the prosecution's case and to mount a defence. All human rights instruments provide that all individuals are to be secure from arbitrary arrest and punishment, are entitled to life, and are to be treated with dignity. Bin Laden is an unappealing candidate for consideration in terms of these provisions. So unappealing, indeed,

DIVIDE AND CANCEL

that when his death – extra-judicial summary execution or war casualty? – occurred, not a murmur was heard about the rule of law and human rights. Bin Laden himself had paid not a jot of attention to such considerations in his commission of mass murders of innocent civilians; why, it can be asked, should he be accorded the privilege of them?

To say this latter, however, is to miss the point. The point is not about the mass murderer and terrorist bin Laden, but about the United States of America, about what sort of state and nation it is. Is it one where vengeance overrides principle? If, as it claims, it is an upholder of the principles of the rule of law and human rights, should it not – for the sake of the future success of these principles in a world in dire need of them – have upheld them, even at the distasteful expense of giving bin Laden his rights together with the great inconvenience of doing so? The short-term gain was great; what about the long-term loss? If bin Laden had been arrested and tried as a common criminal or war criminal, would not the long-term goal of making the world a site of justice and principle have been better served than by acting no differently from Genghis Khan in his heyday?

Conflict makes us forget such questions. Thucydides said that he wrote his history of ancient Greece's Peloponnesian War in part to illustrate this. Early in that war the citizens of Lesbos broke their treaty obligations to Athens and the Athenians decided to punish them in the usual way, which was by killing the men, enslaving the women and children, and destroying the town – that is: by 'cancelling' Lesbos. After a night's reflection they changed their minds, deciding that this was unjustifiably severe. Twelve long years of war later, the island of Melos refused to submit to the Athenians, who did not pause to deliberate whether destroying the Melians was justified, but simply went ahead and did it. In the brief parley beforehand the Athenians warned the Melians that this would happen if they did not submit, saying, 'The right, as the world goes, is only in question between equal powers; otherwise the strong do what they can and the weak suffer what they must.' The Melians are said to have chosen to die as free people rather than live as slaves.[5]

The whole point of the rule of law and human rights is to protect the weak against the strong, in precise refutation of the Athenians' argument to the Melians. Admirers of Nietzsche might see in this the slavish weaklings' conquest of the *Ubermensch* spirit, but all those who have benefitted from the guardianship of these principles against those who are everywhere ever-ready to exploit, expropriate and oppress are glad of them, given the way that power – the power of wealth as well as political power, though these are scarcely distinguishable in practice – so easily corrupts.

And so to the implications of these remarks for the cancel culture issue. The implications concern the question of the principles we are to live by, and what they require of us in the way of balancing short- and long-term gains in matters governed by the principles. We can act in ways that we feel are justified in the circumstances of a moment, only to find that our actions come back to bite us when circumstances change. Principles are very comfortable when they serve us, far less so when they make demands of us that we are emotionally reluctant to meet. Yet they exist precisely because emotions, when they run out of hand, make us do bad and stupid things, sometimes very stupid and very bad. On this view, if in defending the rights of some we deny the rights of others, we thereby do ill.

But this, obviously, depends on answers to the key question of 'rights and wrongs'. Here another lesson from history is appropriate.

In the 1820s white settlers of Tasmania came into violent conflict with the Aboriginal Australian inhabitants of that island in what was labelled the 'Black War'. Hundreds of settlers died in the conflict, and on some estimates perhaps as many as 8,000 Aboriginal Australians. In 1830 the settlers mounted an operation in which 2,000 soldiers and settlers formed a chain and advanced southward across the island in an effort to corral the Aboriginals and – this at least was the most irenic stated intention – 'relocate' them. An incident that occurred in the following year became a *cause célèbre*; the murder by three Aboriginals of two white men, one of whom was especially admired in the settler community – a man called Captain Bartholomew Boyle Thomas, who had been a hero in the Napoleonic Wars and in the liberation movements in South America. A local newspaper, the *Launceston Advertiser*, angrily announced that Boyle Thomas and his estate manager James Parker had been 'barbarously murdered by the inhuman savages ... Thus two more respectable and highly-respected individuals have been added to the list of those who have fallen victims to the barbarity of a race which no kindness can soften, and which nothing short of utter annihilation can subdue.'

Anger at the killing of Boyle Thomas and Parker was exacerbated by the fact that the former, after settling in Tasmania, had been among those who wished to reach a peaceful settlement with the Aboriginal Australians. In a spirit quite opposite to this sentiment, another local newspaper called for Boyle Thomas' death to be avenged not just on the killers 'but upon the whole race'.

The Aboriginals who killed the two men were captured and their guilt was established on the testimony of an Aboriginal woman who had seen the incident. A debate arose as to what was to be done with them. In the course of the debate a remarkable letter appeared in the local press from an anonymous correspondent. The letter's author acknowledged that his or her first reaction was a desire to see 'the extermination of the Blacks', but then serious second thoughts arose – reminiscent of the Athenians and Lesbos – prompting the letter-writer to ask:

> Are these unhappy people the *subjects* of our king, in a state of rebellion? Or are they an injured people, whom we have invaded and with whom we are at war? Are they within the reach of our laws; or are they to be judged by the law of nations? Are they to be viewed in the light of murderers, or as prisoners of war? Have they been guilty of any crime under the law of nations which is punishable by death, or have they only been carrying on a war *in their own way*? ... We are at war with them: they look upon us as enemies – as invaders – as their oppressors and persecutors

– they resist our invasion ... What we call their crime is what in a white man we should call patriotism.[6]

This letter records a *Gestalt* on the part of its writer, suddenly seeing things from a different perspective, a twist of the conceptual kaleidoscope that brings an entirely new picture into view. It takes great maturity of mind and intellectual honesty to achieve a *Gestalt* of this kind, in the midst of fraught circumstances. In the rage of emotion prompted by injustice – injustice that reaches such extremes as the Holocaust of European Jewry in the 1940s; injustice which at the individual level is exemplified by the death of George Floyd on 25 May 2020 at the hands of police in Minneapolis; injustice in its many forms of discrimination, marginalisation and exclusion; injustice in social and economic arrangements that sequester vast wealth and its power into a few hands at the expense of the majority – in the rage of emotion prompted by these things, appeal to 'maturity of mind and intellectual honesty' seems hideously insufficient and misplaced, and instead passion, the energy of anger, direct action, offer themselves as the true and right response.

But – another but – notice something about the litany of injustices just given. To identify the same response as appropriate to all the different examples of it is an obvious mistake. Anger might make it seem appropriate, and it is indeed justified anger; but the 'but' here concerns how it is to be directed and applied. To capture and put to death the perpetrators of the Holocaust, to bring before the law a policeman who uses excessive force motivated by racial prejudice, to organise to change the tax and welfare systems that advantage a plutocracy, to campaign to influence social attitudes towards groups discriminated against, are arguably more appropriate and therefore more effective uses of the anger that these different manifestations of injustice prompt. To the activist burning with fury against injustice – and therefore burning with fury at the unjust people, the unjust system, responsible for it – this seems mealy-mouthed. Not only as a remedy for injustice but as punishment of the unjust themselves, something far more emphatic is desired. And this desire can appear fully to justify the employment of what might in themselves be unjust means.

That describes the situation, or more accurately, the dilemma we face in contemporary society. In the calm of philosophical reflection on these matters a different problem can arise, that of failing to understand the urgency of the passions involved. People are not, as academic assumptions about *homo economicus* wish to have it, agents of unlimitedly rational self-interest. Although one might dispute the idea that reason is never alone the prompt for action – some of the philosophers, notably David Hume, argued this, holding that emotion is indispensable to motivation – nevertheless emotion is far to the fore in this arena. Among these emotions are deep concerns for others, not just kin but individuals and groups on the other side of the world, for animals and natural habitats, for the planet itself. Arguably, the resolve to help, to do something about the bad things that happen, and really to make a difference, requires more than the white heat of anger. 'Everyone can become angry; that's easy; but to be angry with the right person, in the right degree, at the right time, for the right purpose – that is not within everyone's power, and it is not easy', said Aristotle. There is a principle here – let us call it Aristotle's Principle for present purposes – which has to lodge itself at the heart of discussion of these matters.[7] To make good use of it, clarity about what is at issue is essential. The coming pages are an attempt to achieve it.

A point to bear in mind about political debates in general and culture wars in particular is the degree of truth in the following generalisation: that right-wing political movements and especially right-wing political parties tend to be much more unified than left-wing movements and parties. The Right has a set of core concerns around which loyalty congregates, whereas the problems of society and the world are so numerous and diverse that progressives have a tendency to fragment by special interest. Left-wing parties, accordingly, are broader and less integrated coalitions than right-wing parties. This might seem less true now that divisions within the Right in the US and UK have themselves deepened, though much more as a dispute over means than, as is the case with the Left, causes. It would be hard to find a Republican in the US who does not avow commitment to a 'smaller state' (principally meaning lower taxes, less bureaucratic involvement in the economy, immigration anxieties, certain moralistic concerns e.g. on the topics of abortion, marriage and sexual 'deviances', and libertarian latitude in such matters as gun ownership and religion). True enough, almost all on the Left want appropriate taxation to fund central redistribution of social goods to reduce inequality and help the less advantaged, and that is a common cause; but the defence of human rights, the securing of justice and the enhancement of opportunity make many calls across the range of struggles in society, competing for time and resources and sometimes even being inconsistent with each other. The Left has its own divisions over means, from Fabian moderation and incrementalism to street activism. And the urgency and righteousness of many of the causes is a prompt for impatience among the activists, such that the enemy is not the Right – they are merely the opposition – but others on the Left, who are insufficiently active in the activists' view. For their part, the moderates view the activists as self-harmingly misguided in their methods – and thereby harmful to the cause of achieving the goals that both moderates and activists share.

One result of the fissiparous nature of the Left is that the attitudes and practices of the most energetic and vocal come to dominate the scene, with all progressives being painted in the same colours by the Right. In the simplisticisms of the culture war over 'wokism' – this, remember, being a term coined by the Right in disparagement of the excesses, as they see it, of Left campaigns – the danger is that the profoundly important issues at stake are obscured, and efforts to deal with them obstructed, by handing the Right weapons to use in reprisal. Already mentioned is the fact that no-platforming and cancelling employed by some activist groups on the Left have gifted the Right the moral high ground of 'freedom of expression'. Given that – apart from its exceedingly high intrinsic value – this freedom is crucial to the Left for calling out the Right and promoting its causes, this is an own goal of spectacular proportions.

When 'vox pop' surveys are made of conservative attitudes in the US, for example among Donald Trump supporters, the often semi-articulate reasons given for their attitudes include hostility to LGBTQ+, same-sex marriage, gender and transgender debates, reluctance to accept non-binary pronouns like 'they', resistance to efforts in schools to foster more inclusive attitudes, particularly regarding the understanding of racism in US history and society, and more. This right-wing hostility to 'wokism' is often contextualised in the rhetoric of 'Western values' and/or 'Christian values' and beliefs as to what constitutes 'American'. Their source, one is accordingly prompted to think, is anxiety, even fear; a sense of threat. This in turn explains how entrenched such views can be, to the point of ignoring the overwhelming evidence of the unfitness of an individual such as Trump (here another disclosure of point of view) for a position of responsible office.[8] And this in turn again suggests that what one is witnessing is the behaviour of the cornered animal, fear expressing itself as anger and aggression. Holders of such views feel that they are in retreat, losing ground, on insecure footing; the reaction is to fight back.

Couple this with the fact that since the advent of the moving image – cinema and television, and now the 'vlog', TikTok and other visual social media – the mere fact of an individual's visibility, of his or her repeated salience in the public mind, boosts their draw above all other factors.

DISCRIMINATIONS

Familiarity with a face is far more potent than whatever words come out of it, indeed reducing or sometimes obliterating the significance of the words, as politicians like Trump and Boris Johnson illustrate; disconnected sentences conveying no clear meaning, unpleasant remarks, even blatant untruths, have far less effect than sheer recognisability. But if a highly recognisable individual utters phrases that seem to resonate, however inchoately, with those who feel themselves in plight, making him or her seem to be on their side on key issues, almost nothing else matters. The litany of reasons someone opposed to a Trump-like or Johnson-like figure has for that stance gets no traction with their supporters.

Add further that there is much truth in the generalisation that a natural human inclination is to seek leaders, to congregate around someone admired. 'Celebrities' will often observe that fans appear to enter a psychological zone in the presence of their idol, a sort of daze, in which almost all faculties other than a slavish desire for proximity – touching the hem of the robe, so to say – are suspended. Put crudely, humanity divides into sheep and shepherds, and television and visual social media have put even greater mesmeric crooks into shepherds' hands, benign and malign alike. The phenomenon of the 'strong man' leader is a constant in history, but even stark evidence of malign aspects of 'leaders' perceived to be 'strong' is little proof against sheer visibility.

The phenomenon of being cornered, denied, under threat, goes a long way to explaining the adherence of some young males to 'toxic male influencers'. Stereotypes of masculinity and its avocations are challenged by feminism, gay rights, and other trends towards the simultaneous achievement of inclusivity and diversity in society – these not being contradictory, though their opponents' opposite desire requires exclusivity (against perceived Others) for unity (of the tribe). In the case of embattled males in a world aswarm, as they see it, with empowered women, misogyny and anger are the typical response of insecure men, and the attraction of an unrepentant masculinist 'influencer' who thinks women should be confined to the kitchen and submissive to sexual advances is correspondingly great.

Reflection on these considerations is necessary for working out how to overcome the divisions which have, in the increasingly chaotic twenty-first century, become so deep and bitter. The work cannot be one-sided. To protect the achievements of what is, in overall character, the practical application of human rights aims, it is a mistake both in tactics and strategy to make opposition to them even more obdurate – which would be like trying to unblock a drain by impacting the blockage more firmly into it.

***

Engagement in these debates is inevitably complicated by the question of *positionality*. Where is a participant in them 'coming from'? Who and what is that participant, and how might her or his 'position' in race, class, degree of social and economic privilege or lack of it, influence the attitudes taken? It is accordingly not just appropriate but necessary to be as transparent as one can be about one's positionality if one is to stand forward as a participant in these debates.

DISCRIMINATIONS

And when people declare a 'position' one has to be wary about the degree to which – to use the apt term for the case – they 'whitewash' it, putting it in the best light, as often happens in autobiography in general. The whole truth about ourselves is sometimes hard to bear, therefore even harder to reveal. Trying to bear this caveat in mind, my own positionality is as follows.

I am a biological male who has always self-identified as such, born into white privilege, in socially, economically and educationally advantaged circumstances, at a time – in the two decades after 1945 – when almost the entire raft of prejudices that have since been fought against still seemed as natural as breathing to the people who had them. It happens that an early effect on me was a raised awareness of racism. This is because I spent my early years as part of the white expatriate community in parts of Africa (the 'Protectorates' now known as Zambia and Malawi, which were not colonies occupied by white colonisers, such as South Africa, Rhodesia and Kenya) where racist attitudes were less pronounced than in the colonies, though these attitudes most certainly existed; for an example close to home, my own mother was an emphatic racist (my father was not). Because I was brought up by Africans, most dear to me among them 'Johnny' Penza and his first wife Besta, who cared for me when I was little and with whom I spent much of my time, the adverse treatment they experienced troubled me profoundly, and the sentiments thus engendered have not changed. This – acknowledging straight away that few, if any, privileged white people can escape the effect of the structural inequalities that advantage them – went some way to tempering the attitudes that people in such a position then so facilely acquired in their upbringing and circumstances.[9] The generalisation to other social and economic justice considerations followed, so that what in my student days was called 'consciousness raising' was to some degree facilitated. No one can claim to have rooted out all impressions and influences; as with political liberty, the price is eternal vigilance.[10]

My political sympathies are left-leaning, and have leaned further left over time, not – as is supposed to happen with increasing age – the other way, not least because the gains of campaigns for social justice in the 1960s and thereafter have become so threatened in recent decades, or have, deeply dismayingly, turned out to be superficial gains only. I am a committed supporter of human rights, civil liberties and social and economic justice, and can point, as public proof, to many books and scores of articles, written over preceding decades, in vocal advocacy of them. Whatever successes or failures mark my private relationships, I would not lay claim to achievements that anyone who is also an attentive reader (this being one of the chief resources for educating human sympathies) could not claim also.[11]

If there is one thing that I might claim, it is that a commitment to trying to think things through, to respect evidence, to listen to the other side and try to comprehend it and its motivations – not necessarily, and certainly not always, to forgive but just that: to comprehend – has been central to being a philosopher by training and occupation. Given that I can be as enraged by injustice, discrimination, inequality, oppression, cruelty, hypocrisy, dishonesty and manifestations of greed, and by the suffering of the dispossessed and immiserated caused by these things, I find the work of bringing thought to what causes these calamitous features of our world, and how to play some part in remedying them, as arduous as it is for anyone similarly inclined, not least in demanding mastery of the impulse to lash out in the moment. To try to see what is right for individual human beings (and other creatures) where there is a distinction between 'what is right' and 'what I think or wish to be right', and to have deeply meliorist views about public policy questions in the light of structures and realities loaded so heavily in contrary directions, is tough going. But the only alternative to engaging is to shut one's eyes. Alas, many – almost certainly, most: otherwise the world would be a different place – do just that.

It is sometimes argued that people cannot escape their positionality. If that were so, there would be no hope. Too much determinism in this respect forces a hard choice: either you give up trying to make things better, or you have quite literally to extirpate those whose position with its attendant views and practices you oppose. This latter has actually happened so many times in history that one would think lessons should by now have been drawn. One such is that one might find oneself on the losing side, irrespective of the cogency and value of one's own position. That is why the thrust of progressivism in respect of human rights, civil liberties and social and economic justice has been to find a better way between these equally unacceptable alternatives.

***

This book proceeds as follows. To understand properly the universal phenomenon of oppression, subjugation and silencing by one group of another, for which 'cancelling' is an apt general abbreviation, one has to see it at work; and that means not just in contemporary society but in history. The third and fourth chapters respectively give examples of the othering and oppression of groups and individuals. With context and perspective in hand, the succeeding chapters deal with the crucial questions at stake about how the work of combatting injustice is to be done. First, in the chapter immediately following this one, some necessary preliminaries are canvassed, offering perspectives upon key ideas at issue.

2

IDEAS AND ORIENTATIONS

A constellation of concepts recur in the discussion to be had here: 'othering', social exclusion, sin, crime, heresy, punishment, rights, injustice, equality and fairness, freedom of expression, principle, morality, 'cancelling', 'cancel culture' and 'wokeness' – the list is long. This is not a dictionary or an encyclopaedia, but a sense of the most significant concepts, and their relations to each other, is necessary, so this chapter addresses some of them. Considerations of rights, right and wrong, and freedom of expression, are treated more fully later.

In the general background are notions of sin, crime and heresy – things seen as bad and unacceptable – by those opposed to them, and the extension of their meanings to contemporary uses. These are ideas that, in heated circumstances, motivate opposition and repression in most of their forms, acting as drivers to 'othering' others and seeking to 'cancel' them. They are the things whose commission is the target for redress in the form of punishment,

IDEAS AND ORIENTATIONS

restitution or both. Given that what is a *sin* in one person's outlook is a virtue in another person's outlook, that what is to count as a *crime* is a matter of socio-political decision, that the word *heresy* has come to denote any view heterodox with respect to a chosen orthodoxy, the concepts at least require explication. In many if not all societies some sins are treated as crimes and are punishable by law, occasioning a divisive debate about the relation of morality and law. Historically there was often little if any distinction between sins and crimes in those traditions with a concept of sin; the former were simply the latter, and punished accordingly. Separating them has been 'a work', as the French say, 'of long breath'.

***

The concept of sin originates in religious systems, and fundamentally means disobedience to a god or the gods. Metaphors used to describe what the sinner bears as a result include 'stain', 'burden' and 'debt'. In the Judaeo-Christian tradition the first sin, committed by Adam and Eve in the Garden of Eden, was, precisely, disobedience – in eating the forbidden fruit of the Tree of Knowledge. Some glosses specify that the knowledge provided by eating the fruit concerned 'good and evil', but the text of Genesis, chapter 3, implies more general knowledge; Eve, contemplating the fruit's likely tastiness, says that eating it will make her and Adam 'wise' ('a tree to be desired to make one wise', verse 6), and when they ate it 'their eyes were opened' (verse 7).[1] The deity disapproved of their acquisition of knowledge, and visited an extremely heavy punishment on them for it; they were the first victims of Judaeo-Christian cancel culture, driven from the garden, condemned to the sweat of labour for their bread and the agonies of childbirth. In this tradition the history of humankind stems from that act of disobedience; it is the 'original sin' that stains and burdens human nature, so for Christians the redemption and 'atonement' of Christ is essential. His suffering and death repay the debt of sin; sin is the disease for which resubmission to obedience is the cure.

As implied by the gloss specifying that the forbidden fruit conferred knowledge of 'good and evil', the issue is a moral one, and 'what is good' – what is moral – is equivalent to 'obedience to god', whatever god's commands are; for example, an order from the deity to kill one's son (*vide* Abraham and Isaac in Genesis, chapter 22) or slaughter all the inhabitants of a city (*vide* Joshua, chapter 6) makes it a good act, 'acceptable in the eyes of the Lord'.[2] In this view, sin and crime are the same, and the laws and commandments gathered in the first five books of the Hebrew Bible (the Pentateuch) do not distinguish either systematically or clearly between them.[3] Nevertheless a distinction between sins against god and sins against other people is drawn, in that whereas repentance on Yom Kippur, the Day of Atonement, reconciles man to god, reconciliation between one person and another is a separate matter and is not achieved on that day unless the parties come to agreement.

But there are implications for a distinction, albeit ambiguous and inconsistent, in the Hebrew Bible's account of the

613 commandments (the *mitzvot*) and the *halacha* derived from the written and oral Torah. For example, Exodus, chapter 22, verse 1, says, 'If someone steals an ox or a sheep ... the thief must pay back five oxen for the ox and four sheep for the sheep'. This has the character of law, reprising the explicitly legal character of much earlier codes such as that of Hammurabi in the eighteenth century BCE. But the eighth of the Ten Commandments, 'Thou shalt not steal', classifies stealing as a sin, since to steal is to disobey an order from god (Exodus, chapter 20). Scholars suggest that a distinction between sin and crime only began to be formalised in Judaism in the second century BCE.

In Christian moral theology sin came to be viewed explicitly as debt. Translations of the Lord's Prayer offer 'forgive us our trespasses' and 'forgive us our debts' as alternatives; the original meaning of 'trespass' is that of 'tort', a harm done to person or property. According to one scholar the metaphor of sin as a burden or stain came to be replaced by that of debt even in the later layers of the Hebrew Bible and the rabbinic literature of the first centuries CE, though it is principally a view in one major strand of Christianity, reaching an apogee in the writings of St Anselm (d. 1109 CE) – thereby causing the difficulties that subsequently wracked the Reformation between those, viz. Roman Catholics chiefly, who argued that 'works' (works of charity, as a way of repaying the debts of sin) are important to salvation and those, Protestants chiefly, who argued that faith alone (which earns 'grace') is enough.[4]

Protestants in general are inclined to think that all sins are on a par in endangering a believer's relationship with his deity, though some think that once a person has become a committed believer, he is secure in the prospect of salvation, with good behaviour being a grateful response to that fact rather than a way of earning it. Catholics distinguish between venial and mortal sins, the former remediable – they do not sever the individual's relationship with the deity; they include gossiping, drinking too much, telling lies, being covetous – whereas mortal sins are very serious, threatening eternal damnation if committed wilfully and in full knowledge; they include idolatry, blasphemy, adultery, masturbation, and 'sins against faith' such as heresy and not believing in the existence of god.[5] The 'seven deadly sins' are those that are prompts to further sin: pride, greed, lust, envy, gluttony, wrath and sloth. Almost any moral theory, secular or otherwise, might see reason to discourage greed, the wrong kinds of pride, misplaced applications of wrath, and too great a degree of the other sins, so this list is not exclusive to Catholicism or indeed Christianity in general.

Diving into the weeds of these matters is as entertaining as it is fascinating, but a useful closure to the question of how sin differs from crime, together with a characterisation of the latter, is effected by the Catholic priest and former Jesuit David M. Knight in an article in the international edition of the Catholic newspaper *La Croix*, an organ of *halacha* for everyday Catholics.[6] It can scarcely be bettered for directness and simplicity:

> The plain truth is, it is the right and duty of the Church to determine what is a sin. It is the right and duty of the government to

determine what is a crime ... There are all sorts of sins that are not punished as crimes in [the US], from adultery to exploitation of the poor. And the Church has no authority to tell anybody what sins should be punished as crimes. If we allow the Church that right, we are back to the Spanish Inquisition ... The religious affirmation that something is a sin should be guided by a judgment of conscience about right and wrong. It is a moral decision. The political decision to make something a crime should be guided by a practical judgment about what is for the common good. It is a pragmatic decision.

Knight goes on to point out that the founding fathers of the US did not make slavery a crime because doing so would have stopped some colonies voting for independence, while the experience of criminalising what some saw as the sin of alcohol consumption – Prohibition (1920–33) – turned out so disastrously in potentiating other and worse crimes that it had to be reversed. He also reminds us that some laws are positively sinful – in the sense of immoral – such as the Nazis' Nuremberg Laws discriminating against Jews.

'In the sense of immoral'; this phrase reminds us that the idea of sin, originating in specifically religious conceptions of morality, is not – except colloquially – synonymous with 'immoral' in general. A non-religious person might have a clear and coherent set of moral principles which, whether or not they overlap in many respects with tenets of this or that religious morality (succouring widows and orphans, being truthful, keeping promises, etc., are common to almost all religious and non-religious codes alike), do not depend on their being the requirements of a deity, but instead have independent motivation, based on conceptions of what promotes human flourishing and positive social relationships. A secular person is unlikely to call something she regards as immoral a 'sin', except colloquially; but this indicates that to call something a 'sin' in a secular setting, that is, to import the idea of an exacerbated or especially heinous kind of badness in describing something immoral, typically acts as an intensifier of the judgement.

That something – an extramarital affair, say – can be regarded as acceptable by some, as disagreeable by others, as immoral by yet others, and as a sin worthy of punishment ranging from ostracism to death here or damnation in the hereafter (the death penalty for adultery remains an option in at least seven countries at time of writing, and reports that it has been carried out periodically surface),[7] suggests that the labile notion of 'conscience' has the major part in ideas about immorality. Whereas, as often enough happens, a law on a statute book might require interpretation in order to be applicable to the details of a given case, and whereas an injunction in a set of scriptures might have the form, and for some the force, of law, the question of what is immoral or (perhaps even worse, courtesy of the intensification) 'sinful', is something that a person or group can decide and act upon, typically in condemnation of the immoralist as they see him. And this introduces obvious difficulties.

Judgements of conscience are far from invariably arbitrary, however. Consider the thought that there is something wrong in a society that accepts some people having great wealth and living in conspicuous luxury while others sleep on the streets in all weathers. A judgement to that effect will arise from testing the operation of the social, political and economic structures of that society against concepts of fairness, obligations to take into account the interests, needs and legitimate claims of members of the society, and (one hopes) compassion, among which might be the thought that, at very least, equality of opportunity should be a minimum, thus requiring that the society ensures access to education and healthcare for all. The important idea of equality before the law – in practice a dead letter, resort to law being too expensive for most, and very different in its application to rich people and poor people in many countries including the United States and United Kingdom – turns on the idea of 'equal consideration' as a right; but what emerges from political processes are, so often, decisions about the distribution of social goods and entitlements that skew them in practice. Think of the differences between deciding that everyone should pay *the same amount* in tax, that is, a fixed sum, the same for rich and poor – say, $5 from everyone no matter what you have or earn (this is a 'poll tax'); or *the same percentage* – 10% for someone with $100 is $10, for someone with $1,000 is $100; or a *progressively higher percentage* as income and holdings themselves mount, on the grounds that 10% for a poorer person is more of a burden than 20% for a richer person. Each has its proponents, and they all claim 'fairness' and other justifications. Political decisions about these matters accumulate in ways that, in countries like the United States and United Kingdom, result in immense disparities, great wealth reposing in a few hands while others sleep on the street. To judge whether this is acceptable or not – in the latter case not untypically as 'immoral' – is the non-arbitrary outcome of testing the society's structures in the light of value judgements about fairness and entitlement (e.g. to the fruits of one's labours and the legitimacy of inheritance, on the one hand; to human needs and the right to consideration and compassion, on the other). How are such questions to be decided? Either way, the judgements are not arbitrary.

***

Controversy over the relationship between morality and law is perennial. In many societies today, especially in ones that are or verge on being theocracies – that is, where a dominant religious tradition is a powerful influence in society and government – the moral outlook is given legal force; here the concepts of sin and crime overlap or merge. A particular case that illuminates the issues well is the Hart–Devlin debate prompted by the decriminalisation of homosexuality in the United Kingdom.

In 1957 a report, commissioned by the government and known as the 'Wolfenden Report' after its chairman Sir John Wolfenden, was published recommending that 'homosexual behaviour between consenting adults in private should no longer be a criminal offence.'[8] Two years later a senior and influential judge, Lord Devlin, delivered a lecture to the British Academy, later published as *The Enforcement of Morals*, arguing against the report's recommendations.[9] He said that law exists to promote uniformity in society – 'It is generally accepted that some shared morality [is] an essential element of any society' – and that this was the basis on which laws had been enacted against homosexuality because there was a 'strong feeling of disgust in society' against homosexual behaviour, an indication that 'the bounds of [tolerance] are being reached ... No society can do without intolerance, indignation and disgust; they are the forces behind the moral law.' He did not reflect on the significance of the fact that laws against homosexuality as such had been enacted only in 1885, at the height of Victorian moralism, and the 'uniformity' of society which predated their introduction had not until then been sufficient to give legal force to the disgust of the disgusted, though anal sex whether homosexual or heterosexual was illegal and punishable by hanging (the death penalty for this was rescinded in 1861) by a law of 1533.[10] The proscription against anal, or any 'unnatural', sex was ultimately derived from Deuteronomy, chapter 20 (also Leviticus, chapter 20, and Romans, chapter 1).[11]

The philosopher H.L.A. Hart responded to Devlin in his book *The Concept of Law* (1961), arguing that although moral considerations may influence the law, law and morality are different and 'there must remain a realm of private morality or immorality which is, in brief and crude terms, not the law's business'.[12] He cited John Stuart Mill's principle in *On Liberty* (1859): 'the only purpose for which power can be rightfully exercised over any member of a civilized community against his will is to prevent harm to others'.[13] On empirical grounds one can see, Hart pointed out, that law and morality are distinct; laws about registering motor vehicles and prescribing the conditions under which they can and cannot be operated (e.g. blood alcohol limits in drivers, which side of the road to drive on, etc.), are not matters of morality, while moral disagreements over many issues such as abortion, premarital sex, euthanasia, meat-eating, truth-telling in circumstances where harm could result, the limits of loyalty, the death penalty, exist within a single pluralistic society. 'Plural moralities in the conditions of modern large scale societies might perfectly well be mutually tolerant ... there actually are divergent moralities living in peace' not only without the force of law but indeed requiring that none of them be given the force of law to the detriment of others. Elsewhere in his discussion of the question, in particular as applied to abortion, Hart argued in effect that the reverse pressure should be applied; that is, that moral evaluation of laws, not legal enforcement of morals, is appropriate and necessary.

As an example of how in practice such questions play out in society, one notes that the decriminalisation of homosexuality in England and Wales occurred in 1967 – a decade after publication of the Wolfenden Report recommending it – and that in the 1980s conservative reaction to this liberalisation took the form of trying to limit its effects, for example by forbidding schools and local authorities to 'promote' homosexuality (e.g. by neutral discussion of homosexuality in sex education classes; by making publications on homosexuality available in local libraries). This reaction is an instance of a pattern: when advances are made in progressive causes, there will be a counter-campaign, which might take time to develop, sometimes insidiously; consider how, following the achievements of the civil rights and second wave feminism movements of the 1960s and 1970s, a conservative backlash aimed at 'political correctness' emerged in the 1980s and ignited a renewed heightening of conflicts. Today's 'wokism' is a chapter in this story, because of the incompleteness of the gains made by the earlier movements – including real changes in attitudes and practices – and the success of their opponents in maintaining discriminatory structures.

A law–morals conflict essentially identical to the homosexuality debate is that of abortion, manifested in the furore resulting from a Trump-majority Supreme Court in the United States overturning, in its 2022 *Dobbs v Jackson Women's Health Organization* ruling, the 1973 Supreme Court ruling in *Roe v Wade* that abortion is a right under the 'Due Process' clause of the Fourteenth Amendment to the US Constitution.[14] In one way *Roe*'s reliance on this point might appear surprising, given the obvious dangers of 'back-street abortion' and the dire pressures that can force women to choose to terminate pregnancies – both practical considerations. But arguments in favour of a right to abortion in *Roe v Wade* rested in large part on the right to privacy *implied* (not specifically protected) in the Constitution, and its 2022 overturning rested on the justices' claim that the practice of abortion was 'not deeply rooted in this Nation's history or tradition' and was 'not essential to this Nation's scheme of ordered liberty'.[15]

As it happens, the majority decision in *Roe* (written by Justice Harry Blackmun) also cited tradition, stating that abortion did not have 'roots in the English common-law tradition'.[16] But whereas the 2022 decision made crucial use of the 'tradition' argument, the 1973 decision did not; in its case a right to privacy was key. The 2022 argument invoked appeal to tradition as the established and assumedly common moral outlook of a community, while the 1973 reference was to something quite different: the tradition of legal precedent. The 2022 view implies that the mere antiquity of a (moral) tradition is a justification for deciding legality (which would, if pressed to its conclusion, license e.g. criminalising homosexuals and burning people at the stake if they did not share your religious outlook). The 1973 decision relies on a concept – that of privacy – which has moral (more accurately, ethical: see below) grounds that in Hart's fashion are a test of the appropriateness of law and, if anything, deserves legal protection, not the reverse – perhaps at most, as with freedom of expression, requiring qualification for special and defined purposes, and for these only.

Here a direct clash of perceptions is at issue. Privacy, as a right enshrined in human rights instruments such as the UN's 1948 Universal Declaration (Article 12) and by implication in various of the Amendments to the US Constitution, is typically justified by appeal to its importance to individual autonomy, entailing the inviolability of control over one's own body and possessions, one's correspondence, personal data, and home and family life (except for 'lawful' purposes, a qualification added in the UN's 1976 International Covenant on Civil and Political Rights, Article 17). But these justifications in turn rest on assumptions about why these things matter. These are *ethical* assumptions. Ethics – of which moral considerations are a subset – concern the character of what sort of person one is and how one lives.[17] In order to be and to live in a certain way that is one's own choice and responsibility, one has to be autonomous in respects relevant to this. If one lives at the behest and under the control of others, with no choice about what to be and do, one is heteronomous and not a responsible agent – indeed, not an 'agent' at all. Therefore privacy is a fundamental requirement of life as a self-determining individual within the larger constraints of accepting life among others in society, and as having a sphere of action within those constraints that is securely one's own.

Laws criminalising abortion deny the component of that right which gives a woman the autonomy over her body and life to decide whether to carry a pregnancy to term. Since doing the latter is an entire-life-changing matter, this denial is hugely consequential. The 'tradition' invoked by the 2022 Supreme Court is fundamentally one whose moral tenets ultimately take their content, at least implicitly, from the idea that life is god-given and only the deity has the authority to take it away. This is what 'the sanctity of life' means (though it is invoked far less when war and the death penalty are at issue than when foetuses are, the innocence of foetuses contrasting with that of condemned malefactors and enemies in combat). This entails that one's life is not in fact one's own, but belongs to another agency – the deity – and that what one can do with one's life is circumscribed by that fact. For example, religious moralities outlaw choosing to end one's life since one does not own it; proscriptions against suicide have the same ultimate source as anti-abortion views.

The 2022 justices spoke of 'this Nation' as if – against all empirical evidence to the contrary – US society is a single homogeneous thing. Hart's point about moral pluralism is probably more exemplified by the United States than anywhere else on earth. This fact alone should be a reason for not trying to corral the various and disparate populations constituting US society into one mould in every respect, now that the melting-pot ideal – a worthy one in other respects – has failed to be realised, perhaps indeed has been shown to be unrealistic. In the usual way of convenient inconsistencies, other tranches of US public policy are laissez-faire to a fault, especially in economic affairs; the latitude granted to – indeed encouraged in – businessmen in their practices, and the restrictions now reimposed on women in relation to their own bodies, make quite a contrast.[18]

***

The foregoing raises some points to bear in mind about the concepts of sin and crime, and the associated question of the relation between morality and law. Also worth bearing in mind are some points about the concept of 'heresy'.

The word 'heresy' once denoted both a sin and a crime but is now a general label for any view which is deviant either from widely accepted views or strongly held minority views, and – this is an essential component – very unacceptable to those holding these latter.[19]

In fact the word has a benign, indeed positive, origin in ancient Greek *hairesis* which means 'choice'. It described the process by which a student of schools of thought compared them in order to choose one. But it took on its negative meaning in the context of religion, notably in Christianity and Islam, in both of which it has been and can be murderously condemned, though also in Judaism, where it has not been murderous, and Zoroastrianism, where it was occasionally murderous but not to the extent of its principal sites of occurrence in the first two religions. The next chapter recounts some unhappy episodes of extreme cancelling on this basis.

In contemporary parlance the term frequently has positive connotations to denote people who, or ideas which, 'break the mould' – ideas that innovate, introduce fresh perspectives and disrupt orthodoxies in creative and productive ways. But it has also come to denote people who, or ideas which, are strongly unacceptable even to those who are themselves heterodox, who seek to establish their views as the preferred orthodoxy even from their minority standpoint. In this they reprise a feature of religious turmoils involving charges of heresy: the bitterness of division *within* a group, as between different sects of Christians and Muslims, whose closeness in other respects makes the differences between them all the sharper. The familiar joke about the two people who find themselves more and more allied until a final crucial difference emerges goes: 'You're a Label? Great, me too! Are you an A-type Label or a B-type Label? A-type? Wonderful, me too! Are you an AB-type Label or an AC-type Label? AB-type? Super, me too! Are you an ABD-type Label or an ABE-type Label? What!! An ABE-type? Die, you heretic!' The division that has opened within feminism over transwomen and questions of biology and gender is an acute example of this.

***

Those who regard others as sinners or immoralists – and therefore as heretics in the broad sense of enemies of the orthodoxy which judges them so – naturally wish them to stop being that way. This desire ranges from the mere wish that they would stop being objectionable to taking action to oppose them, such action itself ranging all the way from arguing with them to proscribing their activities to killing them – quite a spectrum, and history is full of examples of all these forms. Once opposition to them goes beyond mere wishing, the logic of the situation has a certain dire slope, though it is not necessarily a slippery one; the morals of the offended, or the law, might place limits on where on the slope they stop. But the terrible example of Nazism and the Jews of Europe illustrates the trajectory. From prejudice to calumny and hostility, to proscriptive and discriminatory laws, to physical intimidation and dispossession – the second and third steps aimed at driving Jews away – and at last and worst to mass murder itself, which is the most definitive form of driving away (of cancelling), was a slope descended by the Nazis in a single decade. It is pertinent to keep this worst-case example in mind because the question, 'How far will you go in combatting those whose views, or whom themselves, you find undesirable?' has to be answered when engaging in the combat. In contemporary cancel culture the not infrequent aim is to destroy the reputation and thereby even the career of a person identified as undesirable, which, given that a typical cancel culture social media campaign with this aim is mob justice not due process, raises problematic questions.

And this is because often in such cases the desired outcome is not only protection of those viewed as harmed by the target, but also *punishment* of the target. Repentance by a target persuaded by the justice of the campaigners' cause to change his or her mind and behaviour too often seems insufficient for those whose ire is roused; there must be punishment, the stain is indelible, a soft answer does not turn away their wrath. Avowals of repentance are greeted with scepticism on the grounds that they might be, if not almost certainly are, disingenuous; if so, the perceived danger remains. Cancellation thus tends to admit no appeal. There is rarely escape from mob justice.

These are generalisations, true, but they have an uncomfortable conformity to the facts. To cite contemporary instances is to invite automatic identification with targets, as well as to keep alive cases in which those targets who have been unjustly or excessively victimised are seeking to recover as the storm that broke over them moves away to other and new targets. Because there are so many illustrative cases in the public domain, attention can be directed to that resource in support of the generalisations. It must be added that in plenty of them the campaign is justified; the target really deserved to be called out; but even here questions persist about the punishment aspect of the matter, and about the processes involved.

This, accordingly, invites contemplation of the idea of punishment itself.

***

Punishment is an enormous subject.[20] In summary, the justifications given for punishing wrongdoing – granting that what counts as such has been justifiably identified – are, variously or in combination: deterrence, retribution, rehabilitation, and protection of the community from the wrongdoer.

The deterrent effect is supposed to exist in the threat of punishment if wrong were to be done, or in the warning example to others of a wrongdoer being punished. It is moot whether deterrence is as effective as one would hope. It is hard to say, because plenty of people offend and reoffend despite both the threat and the examples – even the experience – of punishment, while by its nature one cannot know whether wrongs not committed were not committed because someone contemplating doing wrong was put off by the thought of being punished if caught. An aspect of deterrence is the attachment of shame and blame, the denunciation of the wrongdoer as antisocial, meriting the condemnation of society for what he has done.

Retribution is predicated on the idea that wrongdoing must be avenged; the perpetrator must pay by suffering in some respect, typically by being fined or losing freedom but also (in the past and some societies still) by inflictions such as flogging, forced labour, branding or mutilation, or death. Implicit in the etymology of 'retribution' is the idea of compensation; the wrongdoer must restore as much, or yield more, to those harmed than he took from them. But retribution as such does not have to be, and often is not, restorative except in the sense that those harmed take satisfaction in seeing the wrongdoer punished. Relatives of murder victims witness executions in the United States.

A more recent development in liberal societies is the concept of rehabilitation. This involves a twin-track approach; re-educating or treating (by therapy, for example) the offender to address the motivations he had for offending, and equipping him to live without needing to offend upon release. In some cases, controversially, the length of sentence depends upon the degree of an offender's rehabilitation, which places discretion in the hands of those supervising the process. The risk that an offender has skills at appearing plausible, or that a supervisor might take a dislike to an offender, introduces an arbitrariness which does not meet the interests of justice. Some view rehabilitatory approaches, for example giving an offender a non-custodial sentence, as not meeting society's demand that its attitude to the offender and his offence be properly registered.

In general it is thought that the severity of a punishment ought in some way to be commensurate with the gravity of the crime. Unless this were so, a criminal might think that he might as well be hanged for a sheep as for a lamb.* The idea that a group should be punished collectively for what one of

---

* Clothes are hung, people are hanged, a distinction of usage now almost extinct.

its members has done has been a feature of some systems; in ancient Rome if a slave murdered his owner, all the slaves of the household – sometimes numbering in hundreds – were tortured and executed except for any who could show that they strove to prevent the mischief.[21] In most advanced polities this is rightly regarded as unjust.

Controversies over punishment take both empirical and philosophical forms. The empirical considerations relate to the observation that none of the species of punishment seem very effective; the correlation between crime rates and the severity or otherwise of punishments follows no systematic pattern. Severe punishment regimes are not invariably accompanied by low crime rates, nor lenient regimes by high crime rates; increasing and decreasing degrees of punitive severity are not systematically followed by correlative decreases and rises in criminal activity. Countries in which the death penalty is applied have markedly higher murder rates than countries that have abolished it. At most it can be argued that the one invariable effect of sequestering a malefactor in prison, or executing him, is to protect the community from his further depredations.[22]

The moral arguments are more substantive. They turn on the fact that punishment consists in the deliberate infliction of harm in response to the commission of what is socially constructed as a wrong. Both parts of this – 'deliberate infliction of harm' and 'wrongs are socially constructed' – raise questions of their own, and their juxtaposition intensifies the question of what can justify the former. Groups and societies decide what is a crime, and they inflict harm – in the various forms of loss of freedom, distraint of earnings or holdings, death – when they decide that one has been committed. The justifications are those listed above; each regarded as achieving something valuable, this being one or more of reducing crime, taking revenge on the offender, promoting the unlikelihood of reoffence, and keeping society safe.

The objection implicit in the observation that crimes are constituted by social decisions speaks to the fact that deciding to treat something as a crime creates criminals and gives society the authority to punish them. Laws against such drugs as marijuana, cocaine and heroin were introduced in the early twentieth century, creating millions of criminals and placing a massive burden on society to police them. An even more egregious example is Prohibition in the US, placing alcohol consumption in the same category. Some actions and behaviours regarded as crimes – made so by giving moral opposition to them the force of law, for example homosexual sex – have ceased to be so in some jurisdictions, reinforcing the idea that 'crime' is an artefact. At very least these thoughts prompt consideration of the grounds that exist for classifying certain actions and behaviours as criminal, for these grounds have to enter the consequent justification for punishing them.

By no means all such grounds are arbitrary. It would be safe to say that murder and theft are universally acknowledged as unignorable wrongs. In some societies murder was handled by requiring the murderer to recompense the kin of the victim by paying them in money or goods, in most cases on the grounds that the injury was done to the family or clan and not just to the victim. In contemporary Western societies the norm is to treat murder as a crime against the victim and society at large, not specifically to the kin, the unexpressed assumption being that they share with society the compensation represented by the perpetrator's punishment. Theft likewise was dealt with by having the perpetrator repay, or repay with addition, the value of what was stolen. Where thieves were mutilated or branded, a rather different aim was in view: to inflict perpetual shame, to warn others of what mutilation or branding assumes is the irredeemable character of the perpetrator, for these are in their effect life-sentence punishments from which the bearer of the marks cannot recover by any means of reform, regret or compensation. It might be of use to bear this version of punishment in mind since it applies to figurative versions of branding and mutilation also: to cancel someone today is to brand them and socially mutilate them.

It does humankind little credit to note that rape and assault have not shared such universal acknowledgement; in some terminologies the term 'rape' (and 'ravishment') comprehended abduction as well as sexual activity forced against the recipient's consent. Various codes dating from as early as that of Hammurabi designated rape as a crime, while the earliest Common Law provision dates only from the late sixth century CE. The ambiguities in the concept of rape are well exemplified in Roman law on the matter. There, a single defined crime of rape did not exist, but was implied in different ways in conceptions of seduction, abduction and adultery, and depended on the social status of the victim; nonconsensual sex with slaves, sex workers and foreigners was not considered rape, while both consensual and forced sexual congress with citizen women, especially of higher social status, were regarded not only as a violation of their persons but of the dignity of their menfolk and families, and a danger to the integrity of family lines.[23] Women of all classes might have in effect or fact been regarded as chattel in many societies – that is, as a form of property of fathers, husbands or owners; and they still are in some – but not untypically those without the protection of some form of status were regarded as simply available for sexual appropriation as with the classless women of Roman times.[24]

As to assault: it has always been a puzzle to at least this viewer of American cinema that the assault and battery that forms a stock offering of its entertainment seems never to involve charges brought by the victim or the police, as if a punch in the face falls within the accepted range of human interaction. In fact all states of the US classify assault and battery individually or (as in Texas) together as constituting misdemeanours and felonies depending on their gravity (the former carry penalties of up to a year in prison, the latter for periods over a year). The history of these two crimes is interesting in that it originates, in the Common Law tradition, in doctrines of tort (an act or omission that causes harm of a legally recognised kind to persons or property) comprehended under the general label of 'trespass'. As the doctrines developed they fell under the classification of 'intentional torts' along with trespass to land, false imprisonment, fraud and defamation. Assault is the threat, battery the enactment of what is threatened involving physical contact. But battery need consist only in the intentional and offensive touch of a finger on an arm; 'medical battery' occurs when a doctor touches a patient without the patient's permission.

The crimes of murder, rape, theft, and assault and battery are candidates for general agreement, and the fact that they are features of what societies agree to classify as crimes and to merit punishment would be uncontroversial. Far less so are such candidates as homosexuality, consumption of certain drugs – narcotics (opioids), stimulants (methamphetamine, cocaine) and other psychotropics (cannabis, LSD) – refusing to vote, to be vaccinated, to marry, to send your children to school; all of these were once, and are still somewhere, offences under a legal regime.

Some argue that the harms, both intentional and unintentional, done by punishment are ultimately morally unjustifiable, and that wrongdoing should be addressed by dealing with what causes it – inequality, social and economic injustice, society's efforts to corral people into designated channels of behaviour, dysfunctional families, lack of opportunity – and replacing punishment with practices in which offenders compensate victims and are both encouraged and helped to abjure criminality through doing good.[25] The focus is thus on prevention, and rehabilitation when prevention fails. Decriminalising drug *use* and treating its *abuse* as a medical problem (as with alcohol abuse), providing a universal basic income, extending the availability of citizens' advice bureaux to help people deal with problems, having accessible local arbitration and reconciliation facilities, promoting social inclusion, educating to overcome prejudices, and making society a site of fairness overall, would go a long way to cutting all forms of antisocial behaviour including crime. Only for the most serious crimes of murder, rape, fraud, and assault and battery, and for recidivism by offenders – their failure or refusal to take the opportunity to compensate and do better – would the traditional forms of punishment be apt.

Among the reasons for limiting use of imprisonment is the fact that prisons are breeding grounds of crime; 'run with the swift and you run faster, walk with the lame and you learn to limp' is the operative thought here. Prisons are places where criminal alliances can form, methods learned, resentment and hostility to society fostered. The first two could be prevented by keeping all prisoners in solitary confinement; but then the question of further harm being done by that recourse arises; it is a cruel form of punishment – to say nothing of the cost (and cost is far too often the consideration that drives public policy choices).[26]

***

The key pair of notions of direct relevance to the concerns of this book are 'othering' and social exclusion.

Othering is the practice of treating individuals and groups, typically on the basis of stereotyping and prejudice, as a ground for discriminating against them; and discrimination involves exclusion. Political views, religion, sexual orientation, gender, skin colour, ethnicity, nationality and age are the chief targets of otherers. These latter have or adopt an identity viewed as standard, as the norm, and those they treat as 'others' are alien to that norm, licensing a treatment of them as in some way unacceptable to, or lesser than, the home group – 'lesser' in what degree of consideration is to be accorded them.

Extreme forms of othering regard the nominated others as outside the pale of moral consideration, as subhuman, as sufficiently a nuisance or, worse, a danger as to justify treatment ranging from marginalisation and exclusion to punishment, imprisonment, banishment or even extermination. Nazi treatment of Jews, Turkish treatment of Armenians, Hutu treatment of Tutsi, Burmese treatment of the Rohingya, exemplify extreme forms. But all forms of apartheid are classic otherings.[27] Perhaps the most prevalent because endemic forms are racism and sexism. Building walls – China's Great Wall, the wall on the US–Mexico border, the Berlin Wall, the 'peace lines' (fences and walls) in Northern Ireland's towns between Catholic and Protestant areas, the fences and no-go areas between Israel and Palestinian territories – in fact, all national borders, whether marked by walls and fences or not – are physical manifestations of othering. Many if not most borders were drawn in the blood of wars. That none of the walls and fences work has ever dissuaded anyone from erecting them.[28] Almost all conflicts in history and today turn on otherings.[29]

Social exclusion, predicated squarely on othering, consists in the raising of barriers against individuals or groups which prevents them from fully – or at all – benefitting from economic and social life. It is whatever obstructs access to the rights, resources and opportunities required for participation in society, these being the rights and opportunities possessed by the excluders. Obviously, being excluded whether individually or as a group has a generally negative effect, not just on the victims but on society at large, in its turn therefore typically a source of problems – among them crime, and an increased burden on the societies' resources of policing, health and welfare systems; so othering is a costly as well as an unjust matter.

Individuals suffer exclusion when their way of life does not conform to mainstream society's views about norms. Eccentrics, tramps, addicts, criminals are examples. But less obvious situations amount to exclusion; unemployment and disability, poverty, lack of education, have the effect of disabling people from full social membership. Individuals might be excluded not by society as a whole but by groups or entities within it, as when a club blackballs an applicant for membership or a workforce sends a colleague 'to Coventry', a form of ostracism that involves disregarding his presence, not speaking to him or including him. Schoolchildren ganging up on a classmate is another example.

Groups suffer exclusion either through prejudice, as with Roma, or because a society structures itself in ways that do not accommodate one or another minority within them, as with Aboriginal Australians. These two forms of exclusion typically go together; the structures systematically embody the prejudices and give them effect.

Othering differs from social exclusion in one respect, which is that the latter can take the form of conferring invisibility whereas the former turns on a particular perception of the othered. Exclusion disempowers the excluded; othering can do so too but not invariably.

So widespread are othering and social exclusion in human affairs, and so multiple their forms, that entire treatises might be devoted to them. For present purposes one can note that both are often regarded as forms of punishment to be imposed on individuals or groups whose views are rebarbative to the otherers.

Cancelling is both othering and exclusion, and is typically intended as a form of punishment as well as a way of preventing views or practices – those regarded by the cancellers as harmful – from having effect. Cancelling is often enough justified; see below. In difficult cases, where matters are not clear-cut, the question arises about its appropriateness, either altogether or in the degree to which it applies; most particularly, questions arise about the manner in which its appropriateness or degree is arrived at – by due process, or not?

***

A few remarks are required about the terms 'liberal', 'libertarian', 'social justice' and 'wokism', since these have been – no doubt intentionally – muddled, and bear different and competing senses depending on who uses them.

In origin (in the Enlightenment tradition) 'liberal' described an attitude of commitment, at a minimum, to democratic institutions, separation of religion and state, universal human rights, and tolerance. 'Freedom of the individual' is a focus. But the term has come to be considerably muddled by competing interpretations and denigrations; these are discussed in chapter 7 below.

IDEAS AND ORIENTATIONS

'Democratic institutions' embodies the idea that ultimate authority in a state rests in the hands of the people, requiring at very least the following two things: a definition of who 'the people' are, since in every democracy the franchise is restricted e.g. to people above a certain age who are not excluded from the franchise by one or another factor; and a way of ensuring that the 'will' of the people (a complicated idea) can be expressed through institutions and processes of government that are proper and effective, where these last two terms themselves require definition. But the phrase also requires that the people be sufficiently informed, requiring a free press; and that they have the right to assemble and to debate without being gagged or persecuted. At time of writing, democracy is under challenge from both within and without many polities that self-identify as 'democratic'; more on this in chapter 7 below.[30]

The points about democracy's reliance on information, a free and truthful press, and rights to assembly and freedom of expression, explain the commitment to human rights, since the conditions of an open society *essentially* require these elements, along with freedom from enforced adherence to, or overweening influence from, a partisan ideology or a particular religion or creed. The human rights agenda further entails equality of consideration for everyone including racial minorities and LGBTQ+ people.

'Liberalism' came to acquire, as perceived implications of these fundamentals, acceptance of capitalism and private enterprise in some form, what might be described as 'economic secularism'. The difference between European and

US capitalism is considerable; the 'market' in the former is much more regulated than in the latter as regards control of quality of goods, temptations to manipulation such as monopolies and price-gouging, consumers' rights, taxation of profits and dividends, and more. Taxation, as a means of redistribution by providing social goods of health and education and the enablement of opportunities these provide, together with a welfare safety net for those who struggle, is regarded as justified; it is seen as the society co-operating, pooling part of its resources, to enhance its overall quality of life. These ideas are regarded as considerably less persuasive in US capitalism. Indeed, in the rhetoric of opposition to liberalism, in this sense, in the US, it is often demonised as 'socialism' therefore.

There are several versions of socialism, some not very different in most essentials from liberalism, except that a major differentiator is the commitment in socialism to an extensive degree of control, preferably public ownership, of the means of production, distribution and exchange in the economy, and its emphasis on the class divisions in society forced by the economy's capitalist structure. In practice economic management in polities claiming to be genuinely socialist has too often extended, by necessity given the difficulties encountered, into control of the population by denying some or all of the human rights and civil liberties distinctive of liberalism.[31] Besides the coercive control of the population required for it, fully centralised management of the economy has proved a failure too, wherever it has so far been tried. This point is consistently ignored by those who use 'liberal' pejoratively as a synonym of 'socialist' in American political discourse. China has succeeded in achieving massive economic growth by retaining stringent social and political control but greatly modifying the operation of its economy, sometimes described as a 'mixed socialist market' model.

'Neoliberalism' focuses on a version of capitalism not predicated on the idea that some common pooling of resources to achieve social justice is justified – though it accepts it for policing and defence. Neoliberalism is not liberalism but *libertarianism*, a very different animal. Its use of the phrase 'freedom of the individual' applies most especially to economic agency; it is in favour of deregulation, privatisation, the lowest possible levels of taxation, and leaving outcomes to be decided by market forces, *caveat emptor*: let the buyer beware. Education and health are to be bought at one's own expense, if one can afford them, regarded not as social but as private goods. Seeking and making opportunities are the individual's responsibility, and the rewards for success are the individual's own, and should not be taxed to pay for what others should pay for out of their own pockets. As Margaret Thatcher famously put it in articulating this view, 'There is no such thing as society'. Whereas liberals regard the effects of large inequalities in social and economic terms as depriving many – and usually most – of significant aspects of individual freedom, neoliberals in effect reserve freedom to those able to buy it.

Liberalism places opposition to social injustices and inequalities of concern and opportunity among its central preoccupations; these are what the idea of human rights seeks to combat. Neoliberalism is hostile to ideas of equality and social justice. But the term 'social justice' itself has undergone a transmutation, as a result – so some argue – of 'postmodernism'. A feature of this '-ism' is the rejection by some of its leading proponents of the idea that there are such things as 'objective truth' or 'factual knowledge', arguing instead that these are partisan constructs decided by those in power – not just governmental power with its control of the instruments of force in society, but ideological power in general.[32] The point is sometimes put by saying that reality is the product of discourses, different discourses projecting different realities.[33] This relativism seems to present a problem to the postmodernist, critics say, for it contradicts the idea that there are objective values of equality and social justice which ought to be realised in society. What this suggests is that those who begin with the postmodern analysis of objectivity and knowledge are not actually saying that there are no such things, but that how they have been constituted in the past should be replaced by new and better conceptions of them. This raises the question of who is to be the authority saying what they are. In line with the justification for the concept of human rights – viz. the facts attendant upon their absence – the same might be offered in reply here: that the experience of the marginalised, excluded and discriminated-against tells us.

However, one feature of the development of ideas about 'rights' in the postmodern era is that it has been expanded from *individual* to *group* rights, and from there in turn to questions of *identity*. Here problems arise; but the move underlies a consideration that has independent force. It is the idea that racist or sexist prejudice does not consist only in what one person displays in discriminating against another of a different race or gender, but that it is systemic, diffused throughout society and its institutions. A classic statement of this observation is Peggy McIntosh's 'White Privilege: Unpacking the Invisible Knapsack', first published in 1989 and widely influential.[34] There is much right about this. But the argument goes further; that such discrimination is often invisible to all but its victims or those with a consciousness sufficiently raised to perceive it. This results in the view that those in a position to recognise even the subtlest manifestations of racism or sexism in others' words or behaviour, and microaggressions arising from them, are the authority on their occurrence; the manifestations occur if the victims say that they occur. There is much right about this too. But there is also an obvious danger in it.

'Identity politics' is a phrase that captures a major implication of the idea of group rights. The chief foci around which debate rages are accordingly race, sex and gender, and sexuality; identity collectives. The old liberal value of autonomy is, perhaps paradoxically, invoked in providing unrestricted latitude to *self*-identifying as a member of one or other of these collectives, although the idea of 'appropriation' sometimes obstructs efforts to do so, as for example in cases where people, castigated as 'Pretendians', claim an identity that others (of that identity) refuse to accord them.[35] Appropriation disputes arise also when, say, an author who is a member of one racial group makes a character in her novel a member of another racial group, or an actor plays the part of someone from another racial group.

Identity politics activists are those whom conservatives include centrally under the 'wokist' label as, in their passion for their causes, they variously promote their views by all or some of Critical Race Theory in history classes, campaigning for same-sex marriage, educating about diversity in sexuality, supporting medical gender transition, advocating changes in language use such as employing 'they' in place of 'he' and 'she', avoiding expressions prefixing or suffixing 'man' or 'men', rejecting the tradition that semantically 'man' denotes 'human being', and – in the case of feminist action – encouraging Me Too avowals.[36] At the same time a significant number of them promote no-platforming and cancellation as weapons in the struggle.

Critics particularly identify negatives in this last. Because use of these weapons yields the 'freedom of expression' high ground to the Right, it causes a quarrel between people on the same 'woke'-*goals* side about *methods* and *means*, and the way that perceived excesses by activists have driven some who were, or remain, on the 'woke' side into becoming fellow-travellers with the Right in regard to those means and methods. The examples of the Columbia University linguist John McWhorter, and the liberal comedian and talk show host Bill Maher being quoted with approval by Fox News for inveighing against activist excesses, are two of many.[37]

It is both interesting and relevant to note what the Pew Research Center found in 2021 in polling people on attitudes to 'cancel culture'. As one would expect, the division ran down

Right–Left lines: 'Where Some See Calls for Accountability, Others See Censorship, Punishment'.[38] Around half of those polled had heard of cancel culture; nearly half of these again defined it as action to hold others accountable. Taking just those who had heard of the term, some said such action could be 'misplaced, ineffective or overtly cruel'; 14% described it as censorship, restricting free speech and erasing history, and 12% as 'mean-spirited attacks used to cause others harm'. A third of conservative Republicans and half of liberal Republicans took the 'holding accountable' definition to apply, compared to 54% of conservative Democrats and 59% of liberal Democrats. Conservative Republicans viewed cancellation as censorship at a rate between two and three times greater than Democrats.

The view that calling people out on social media for offensive posts justifiably holds them to account was held by 75% of Democrats and 39% of Republicans, while 56% of Republicans and 22% of Democrats believed that 'this type of action generally punishes people who don't deserve it'. An odd asymmetry between Left and Right is that less well-educated Republicans are more likely to see cancellation as holding people accountable than better-educated Republicans, while the reverse is true for Democrats. Perhaps most interesting are the replies quoted in Pew's report to the questions 'Why is cancellation accountability?' and 'Why is cancellation punishment?', asked of the respective attitude-holders. A number of them are thoughtful and nuanced, and repay reading.

***

It is vital to remember that among those called out and challenged by activists are many who demonstrably need to be called out and challenged. Egregious examples like Harvey Weinstein make the case. Some activists could be imagined as arguing against the criticism that the net is flung too wide and some of the targeting is therefore unjust by saying that collateral damage is expected in war. This is an 'ends justify the means' argument. Not all applications of this argument pass muster; on which, more later.

It is also vital to remember that to criticise the means chosen by activists can be interpreted as 'punching down' in response to their 'punching up' against people and institutions often with power and influence, and in addition can be interpreted as defending the challenged. It should not be the first and should only be the second if justified, which – to repeat – is not always the case. This connects with what is thought to be the origin of the term 'woke' itself; that it arose in the tradition of Black consciousness as a rallying cry to wake up to injustice and stay awake. It would seem to any dispassionate person that being fully awake to the existence, sources and nature of injustice in the world is everyone's duty.

In the case of culture wars and 'wokism' in the first third of the twenty-first century, the application of human rights protections in matters of race, reproductive rights, sexuality, sex and gender should be uncontroversial, but they are not; the effect of conservative defence of 'Western liberal values', especially as conducted by those on the further Right of that spectrum, too readily looks like a mission to deny equal access to public life and acceptance of women, LGBTQ+ communities and ethnic minorities, by denying them the full application of what regimes of rights are designed to provide. On the other side of the conflict, most if not all 'wokism', indeed most if not all ambition in these matters on the Left in general, consists in endeavours to assert and protect these rights. But the conflict's battle lines are not a simple binary; to the advantage of the Right, the Left is divided within itself over methods. Despite widespread agreement on goals on the Left, disagreement over means has opened a gulf between moderates and activists.

Disagreement over means focuses chiefly on 'no-platforming' and 'cancelling'. It has to be repeated, again, that there are plenty of cases where they are individually or jointly justified. To refuse a platform to hate speech is justified, defining 'hate speech' as discriminatory, derogatory or inciting speech directed against individuals or groups on grounds of race, sex, gender, disability or age.[39] Such speech is indeed criminalised in some jurisdictions, a socially based decision to 'no-platform' it conclusively. Difficulties arise when one side of a dispute about what is to be acceptable defines 'hate speech' according to its own stance; this is a matter for case-by-case justification. To cancel individuals is also justified in many cases; people whose position requires of them that they behave (speech is behaviour) in non-discriminatory ways but who say or do things that reveal discriminatory attitudes deserve to be called out and if necessary deprived of that position, since their occupancy of it could or does cause harm. Given that 'position' here covers a wide range, the justification for cancelling such people is also, indeed very much, a case-by-case matter. Positions of influence or authority are especially relevant.

DISCRIMINATIONS

A sexist schoolteacher, a politician who is heard to express racist views, a television news presenter who is heard to make discriminatory remarks about elderly or disabled people, anyone in a position of power relative to others who uses that power to sexually harass and exploit, are legitimate targets not just for criticism but for questions about their suitability for their roles. Calls to remove them from those roles in egregious cases are justified; the last example is a paradigm of this.

Difficulties arise on the more ambiguous margins of these matters.[40] One party might apply, or extend, the definition of what is unacceptable in ways that catch other parties in their 'cancelling' net without such a clear-cut justification. This problem is exacerbated by the fact that cancelling campaigns are frequently conducted through social media 'pile-ons' which, in lacking due process and a considered application of the principle *audi alteram partem* ('hear the other side') can at their worst exemplify the pattern of mob justice, a lynching process where the campaigners are prosecution, judge and executioner in one.

When this happens, 'no-platforming' and 'cancelling' gift the opponents of social justice movements the 'free speech' high ground. The understandable frustration and anger of woke campaigners who feel that their arguments are being dismissed, their claims denied, and the structures of society barricaded against them, can seem or be made to seem shrill and violent, again giving those who benefit from social injustices, safely lodged behind their barricades, weapons to use against the campaigners. Indeed: were I a Machiavellian I would disrupt campaigners' endeavours by employing actors to pretend to be social justice warriors, but in such a way as to caricature the endeavour by extreme pronouncements and actions, thus discrediting it. Similarly I would disrupt a demonstration in support of some good cause by employing a few thugs to join it and to spend their time breaking windows and knocking off policemen's hats, for the media would pay exclusive attention to these events – drama equals viewer and reader numbers; like dogs chasing squirrels, that is the media reflex – and the message of the demonstration would be marginalised or drowned. It is sometimes a temptation to wonder whether 'the Bannon playbook' on how to subvert the enemy is in operation in such cases.[41]

Granting that 'no-platforming' and 'cancelling' are often justified, and when so are powerful weapons for social justice endeavours, one has to remain alert to their dangers. The dangers are in full view; most social justice campaigners are – or for most of their history were – victims of 'no-platforming' and 'cancelling' themselves, and well know what being subjected to them is like. They were denied a voice, denied a full place, denied opportunities, by no-platformers and cancellers in opposing groups, the latter frequently constituting the privileged ranks of society. Some therefore might feel that 'an eye for an eye' is justified. To see what this can lead to, I think it is vital to know the history of cancelling and the excesses it can involve. The next two chapters survey that history, to set the context for discussing how things might be done differently, and in the process to warn against extremes.

3

OTHERING, EXCLUDING AND CANCELLING *GROUPS*

It could be argued that subjugation, overmastering, oppressing, even to the point of actual or attempted extermination, by one group of another, is the theme of history itself. War is an obvious example. Attempts less than outright war are even more numerous. Merely mentioning the names by which the more infamous examples are known – *vide* 'Holocaust' – would make the point, especially if so chosen that one could see how, in approving of some and disapproving of others, we would learn some lessons about why mutual tolerance is regarded as a virtue even on the prudential grounds that you and I almost certainly belong to groups that some other groups would like to see cancelled. After all, conservatives would like to see 'wokists' cancelled, in the sense of *silenced* and *marginalised*.

In insisting that some things should absolutely not be tolerated – murder and rape are uncontroversial examples – one has also to insist, in parallel to the saying 'an open mind is a good thing, but not so open that your brains fall out', that one's disapprovals, if they are to justify suppressing views, groups or persons that one disapproves of, have to have as good a case to make as for uncontroversial examples.

Just mentioning infamous examples of historical oppressions leaves out the reasons and motives on the oppressing and oppressed sides that prompted them. It is from the details that lessons are to be derived. Chief among the motives for considering the details is seeing why oppressors were provoked enough to do what they did. Although the French say *tout comprendre c'est tout pardonner*, 'to understand all is to forgive all', this is not true; to understand is not automatically to forgive, indeed it might be a reason for being even less inclined to forgive. But to understand is key. In cases where understanding deepens one's opposition to acts of oppression, one finds the best grounds for being thus opposed, in the process enriching the case for one's principles.

There are so many examples of oppressions and suppressions, otherings and excludings, massacres and genocides, that mere mention of those already cited – e.g. Armenians, Rohingya, Tutsi, and above all, fifteen centuries of antisemitism and the nadir of its many nadirs, the Holocaust – should be enough. But for the detail of sentiments involved, the following examples are illustrative. In reading them, the echoes of even less murderous culture wars are to be noted.

Focus on the details of one such example: the suppression of Catharism in Languedoc (southern France) in the twelfth and thirteenth centuries CE. This violent series of actions against a religious group regarded as aberrant by the Church was the proximate cause, the beginning, of the assorted phenomena collected under the label 'the medieval Inquisition'. Scholarship has shown that until after 1200 CE there was no central organisation meriting that name, but a number of different local actions, and that in the early modern period (from the fourteenth century CE) the Inquisition in Spain, Portugal, Venice and Rome took different forms. In the first of these two places especially it reached levels of persecution that prompted later critics of the Church (i.e. the Latin Church; what after the Reformation came to be called the Roman Catholic Church) to lump all the inquisitorial phenomena under a single label *The Inquisition* as an horrendous example of bloody persecution.[1] In enough cases Inquisitions were indeed so, representing a coercive endeavour to stamp out heterodoxy and impose the authority of the Church in doctrinal matters; and thousands were tortured and burned at the stake. But although serious questions arise about the judicial methods employed by inquisitors, in most cases they followed a pattern of investigation first established by the magistracy in Roman Imperial times. This was not a mere matter of form; estimates now have it that those put to death under Inquisitorial judgement represented about 2% of those investigated, and there was opposition to these practices from within the Church itself.[2] The excesses of the Spanish Inquisition, initiated by Tomas de Torquemada, came to colour the whole concept of the process; but the argument of the Church itself (*vide* the account in the *Catholic Encyclopedia*)[3] and scholars such as Edward Peters,[4] that the Inquisitions were not quite as bad as their critics made out, does not mask the fact that the endeavour was to root out dissent and impose orthodoxy, in the extreme by execution. It is a luminous example of cancellation at work, and the extremes to which it can go.

The immediate trigger for persecution of the Cathars was the murder in 1208 of a Cistercian monk called Pierre de Castelnau, who had been sent by Pope Innocent III to the ruler of the Cathar region, Raymond VI Count of Toulouse, to get the latter to suppress Catharism. Until then the Church had attempted to reconvert Cathars by means of persuasion and discussion. These efforts failed, hence Castelnau's more minatory approach. After angry exchanges between them, Castelnau excommunicated Raymond and set off back to Rome. *En route* he was murdered, presumably by one of Raymond's retainers. This prompted Innocent III to exhort King Philip II of France to mount a crusade against the Cathars, offering as an inducement permission to the crusaders to take ownership of lands liberated from Cathars and those (the Languedocian nobles) who protected them. This was temptation enough for the northern French nobles, who therefore gathered forces of soldiers, mercenaries and pilgrims at Lyon and embarked on what came to be known as the Albigensian Crusade, named for one of the strongholds of Catharism, the town of Albi.

The crusade's leaders were impelled as much if not more by the prospect of plunder than religious zeal, but the Pope made use of that motive, and the crusade's overall commander was the papal legate Arnaud Amaury, abbot of Citeaux. The first major incident was the massacre of the population of Béziers on 22 July 1209. The crusaders laid siege to Béziers; an attempted sortie by the town's defenders failed, and they were so hotly pursued as they fled back through the gates that crusaders were simply able to follow them in. Famously, or infamously, when asked how his troops were to distinguish between Catholics and Cathars, Amaury is alleged to have said, 'Kill them all, God will know his own.'

The crusaders slaughtered men, women and children indiscriminately, dragging them from the sanctuary of churches and killing them in private houses and the streets, and then set the town ablaze. Amaury wrote to Pope Innocent, 'Our men spared no one, irrespective of rank, sex or age, and put to the sword almost 20,000 people. After this great slaughter the whole city was despoiled and burnt, as divine vengeance miraculously raged against it.'[5] In the *Historia Albigensis* by Amaury's fellow-Cistercian, Peter of Vaux-de-Cernay, the justification is given: he described Béziers as 'entirely infected by the poison of heresy' and 'overflowing with every kind of sin'.

Without question the following twenty years of war between the crusaders and Languedoc's nobles and people had a large element of economic and political motivation; the war brought the region fully into France, having hitherto been a constellation of independent princedoms (though notionally under the suzerainty of the French monarchy), and crusader leaders like Simon de Montfort gained rich landholdings from it. But the religious motivation was key, both as excuse and aim. This is shown by what was at stake in doctrinal terms.

Consider the position of the Church. Its attitude can be well summarised by the premise on which it still stands today

– *semper idem*, 'forever the same': 'Religious belief is something objective, the gift of God, and therefore outside the realm of free private judgment ... the Church is a society perfect and sovereign, based substantially on a pure and authentic Revelation, whose first most important duty must naturally be to retain unsullied this original deposit of faith ... that orthodoxy should be maintained at any cost [is] self-evident.'[6]

The key commitments of this doctrine include the one-in-three-persons of God the Father, Jesus Christ his son and the Holy Ghost (the Holy Trinity); Christ – though of one substance with the Father – being incarnated by means of the virgin parturition of Mary and suffering, dying and resurrecting salvifically; the Church is the Body of Christ, and contains and administers (including developing) the teachings with which it is entrusted; there will be a Last Judgement of Christ, and via the remission of sins the Life Everlasting can be attained. Participation in the sacraments of baptism, the Mass, marriage and Extreme Unction are key components.

Compare the doctrine of the Cathars. Their name comes from *katharoi*, 'pure people'. Their own name for themselves was 'Good Christians'. Fundamental to their outlook was the belief that there are two gods, the good god of heaven and the wicked god of this world. The principal source of this belief lay as far back as Manichaeism with its dualistic conception of the world as a struggle between the powers of good and evil – between Light and Dark – probably transmitted to Western Christendom through the Bogomils of Bulgaria in the tenth century CE. Empirical evidence – just looking about one – is enough to suggest that the world is under malign government, but the Cathars had scriptural justification too; for example 2 Corinthians, chapter 4, verse 4, says, 'The god of this world hath blinded the minds of them which believe not, lest the light of the glorious gospel of Christ, who is the image of God, should shine upon them.'

The god of this world, 'Rex Mundi', was identified by Cathars with the god of the Jews in the Old Testament, and with Satan. They believed that the evil in human experience arises from the fact that the two gods are so nearly equal in power that each limits what the other can do.[7] The evil god created matter in which to trap both the spirits and souls (two different things for Cathars) of angels who were misled into rebellion against the good god. Although Cathars worshipped Jesus and cleaved to what they regarded as his 'true teachings', they rejected the ideas of his incarnation and resurrection – how could a divine being take on evil matter? – sharing with Docetists the belief that he was an angel disguised as a human, his apparent human materiality an illusion.

Along with other trappings of the orthodox story, Cathars rejected the symbol of the cross, representing as it does a torture instrument that only works in material terms, and likewise baptism – because water, a material substance, cannot endow spiritual blessings. Accordingly they also rejected the baptiser himself, John the Baptist, indeed seeing him as evil because his intervention threatens to mislead people about Jesus's true nature. The *perfecti* – those Cathars who applied in full this theology to their lives – regarded sexual attractiveness, especially of women, as a barrier to escaping the material world, so they abjured sex, and would not eat anything that resulted from sexual intercourse, not just animal flesh but eggs and milk. They were pescatarian, however, because they thought fish and shellfish were spontaneously generated. Those Cathars who could not forgo sex or meat had to hope that in some successive reincarnation – this being another element of Cathar theory – they might be strong enough to achieve the status of *perfecti*. Like the Pythagoreans they believed that human souls could reincarnate into animals. Cathars were against killing in any form – hence a second reason for not butchering animals – and because they believed that spirit is genderless, women had greater equality and autonomy in Cathar society – this included being *perfecti*, which was the closest thing in an otherwise unhierarchical society to being priests and bishops able to administer the chief sacrament of Catharism, the *consolamentum*, a form of Last Rite, which believers hoped would advance them to a perfected state.

Juxtaposing Catholic doctrine alongside the beliefs of the Cathars is enough to show how intolerable they are to each other. One can add, if only to leave aside, the thought that the comfortable, even luxurious, lifestyle of Church dignitaries would be challenged by the asceticism of Catharism, to the prelates' annoyance and discomfiture. But the doctrinal divide is so great, and the degree of logic evident in the Cathar reading of texts and traditions too divergent, to allow anything but the eventual thought, 'It's you or me; one of us must go'.

Naturally, both sides regarded the other as heretics. In his letter to King Philip urging him to mount a crusade against the Cathars, Innocent III wrote that 'the plague of heresy and the madness of our enemies has gone from strength to strength ... do not delay in opposing these great evils ... Work to root out perfidious heresy in whatever way God reveals to you. Attack the followers of heresy more vigorously even than the Saracens, for they are more evil'.[8]

The Cathars could point to the absence of a scriptural basis for the doctrine of the Trinity; the frequent drawing of a contrast, in the Gospels, between this world and the Kingdom of Heaven as two domains over the former of which the Prince of Darkness has been given rule; the wickedness of the repeatedly genocidal deity of the Old Testament and that book's appalling morals, exemplified by Abraham having issue from a slave; the Levites slaughtering 3,000 Israelites who worshipped the Golden Calf; Lot offering his daughters to be ravished by the mob in Sodom and later fathering children with them; Joshua massacring the inhabitants of Jericho; David seducing Bathsheba (first sending her husband to the front lines in battle to get him out of the way); Solomon with his thousand concubines; Elisha cursing the youths who mocked his baldness and causing two bears to tear forty-two of them to pieces – to say nothing of animal sacrifice, circumcision, and the general terrorisation by their god of his chosen people. The Cathars had a point.

Because the option of a *convivencia* – the state of mutual tolerance that, for a prime example, existed in practice in Spain among Christians, Jews and Muslims from the eighth century until the time of Ferdinand and Isabella and the conclusion of the *Reconquista* in the fifteenth century – was no longer seen as an option, cancellation was the logical alternative for the Church, now that it had the power to enact it. Christianity had struggled with heresy from close to the beginning of its history. Gnostics, Arians, Nestorians, Docetists, Adoptionists, Sabellians, Montanists, Pelagians, Donatists, Marcionites and others all had their own interpretations and variations, and the effort to establish a unified orthodoxy in Christianity's early centuries was a difficult one. In the end the Great Schism of the eleventh century CE between Latin and Greek Christianity – Western and Eastern – turned ultimately on the word 'and' (the *que* in *filioque* – 'and the son') – although of course there were political and economic reasons too, the Eastern churches resenting the claims of the Pope in Rome to exert authority over them. But 'and' was the doctrinal reason: the Romans wished to include it in the Nicene Creed to make Jesus coequal in divinity with the Father, in order that the Holy Ghost can 'proceed from the Father *and* the Son' – this to combat the Arian view that the son is lesser than the father. It was controversial within the Western church itself until Pope Benedict VIII decreed in 1024 that 'and' must be in the Creed, thus triggering the rupture with the Eastern church.

But in the period from the second to the thirteenth centuries heresy disputes had not involved persecutions and pogroms; they had principally taken the form of written and *viva voce* quarrels, and it was rare for the Church to hand delinquents to the temporal powers for punishment. The marked change occurred with Innocent III. He wrote, 'We affirm that the secular power can, without mortal sin, exercise judgment of blood, provided that the sentencing was made not by hatred, but by judgment.' Concurring, Thomas Aquinas wrote, 'If any individual becomes a danger to society and if his sin is contagious to others, it is laudable and beneficial to put him to death on behalf of the common good.'[9]

Heresy was adjudged a crime because it impugned the true word of God, because it threatened the souls of those who might be led astray by it, and because it challenged the authority and unity of the Church. Among the justifications for inflicting the ultimate penalty on heretics who would not recant was the idea that by shortening their lives the Church was preventing them from adding yet more sins to their souls, thereby shortening their sojourn in Purgatory; in that sense it was doing them a favour. One would guess that few, as the flames rose about them on the stake, saw it that way.

There is a trajectory in the Church's history of dealing with heresy. In the early centuries Christians debated internally about the right interpretation of their faith, and the Church Fathers wrote also to persuade a sceptical and diverse Roman Empire of the truth of their religion, this endeavour known as 'apologetics'. With Innocent III the Church had reached a point where its power and influence enabled it to abandon persuasion for command and, wherever necessary, coercion. Persecution, torture and the stake became instruments of orthodoxy. By the Enlightenment of the eighteenth century, following the Reformation and the widespread social and intellectual changes that followed, the Church could no longer dictate what people should believe and kill them if they disagreed (Giordano Bruno and Cesare Guilio Vanini at the beginning of the seventeenth century were among the last to be burned at the stake for heresy; Galileo came close to the same fate),[10] so apologetics had again to be resorted to; William Paley's *Evidences of Christianity* (1794) is an example. Excommunication – exclusion, not infrequently with dire consequences of its own – was the form of cancelling that predated and followed the more emphatic version of cancelling by killing.

This trajectory – impatience arising from the failure to persuade by argument – is a warning. It has been exemplified in so many cases that it is or should be a *dire* warning. But this is not the only way that oppression and suppression arise. The grounds on which some forms of othering occur do not admit of the possibility of persuasion; a racist cannot persuade a person of a different 'race' to become one of his own 'race'.[11] Here other factors are in play driving prejudice, discrimination and cancelling by oppression and suppression.

The number of times cities and their populations have been subjected to the same treatment as Béziers is unknown but very large, and not all of them were prompted by doctrinal differences. The sack of Magdeburg (an estimated 20–30,000 killed) on 20 May 1631 did have doctrinal prompts; the commander of the Catholic forces that attacked the Protestant city, Graf Gottfried Heinrich zu Pappenheim (a convert to Catholicism), wrote afterwards, 'I believe that over twenty thousand souls were lost. It is certain that no more terrible work and divine punishment has been seen since the destruction of Jerusalem. All of our soldiers became rich. God with us.'[12] Magdeburg was the city from which the first major doctrinal text of Lutherism, the Magdeburg Confession of 1550, came; it thus occupied a signal place in newly Protestant parts of Europe – therefore deserving, so the Catholic army thought, punishment. But Genghis Khan's destruction of Samarkand in 1220, in which the entire population was slaughtered and their heads piled into a huge pyramid outside the city, had nothing to do with religious doctrines; instead it was designed to terrorise opponents – a frightened enemy is a weaker enemy; an example of psychological warfare – as well as securing the Mongol lines of communication, leaving no enemies in the wake of the army.[13]

Samarkand, therefore, was an example of practicality, of which the 'area bombing' of civilian populations in the Second World War is yet another.[14] Nevertheless both are cases of othering and cancellation. Reasons might differ; the effects are terribly the same. In 'Operation Gomorrah', the bombing of Hamburg by 3,000 RAF bombers over four nights (24, 27, 29 July and 2 August 1943), 46,000 people died, many of them in the horrendous firestorm on the second night of attack, in which bodies were shrunk to the size of dolls by the heat, people were asphyxiated in bomb shelters because all the oxygen was sucked out of the air, those who leapt into canals to extinguish splashes on them of a form of napalm used in incendiary bombs found that it spontaneously reignited when they got out of the water.[15]

***

OTHERING, EXCLUDING AND CANCELLING *GROUPS*

In the cases of both Stalin's attack on Ukraine's kulaks and China's Cultural Revolution the motive was not religion or ethnicity but ideological enforcement. Stalin declared the kulaks – independent Ukrainian farmers who resisted imposed collectivisation – 'enemies of the people' and said they must be 'liquidated as a class', which he achieved by forcing the country into famine. On some estimates seven million died of starvation between 1931 and 1933; all the grain was taken to Russia, animals were fed instead of people, desperate mothers flung their starving children onto trains heading towards Kyiv in the hope that someone there would find them and feed them.[16]

Mao's 'Great Proletarian Cultural Revolution', launched in 1966, was aimed at expunging capitalist and traditional features of Chinese society – the 'Four Olds': 'old habits, old ideas, old customs, old culture' – but was also a move by Mao to regain power because he had been partly sidelined after the disaster of the Great Leap Forward (1958–62) and the famine it caused, responsible for the deaths of between 15 and 55 million people, depending on which estimate one accepts. In the chaotic conditions of the Cultural Revolution a further one to two million were killed in acts of mob violence, notably in the provinces of Guangxi, Guangdong, Hunan, Inner Mongolia and in the city of Beijing itself. According to Lebin Yan, a participant in the events in Guangxi Province, as many as 150,000 people were killed by beheading, disembowelling, stoning, beating, drowning or live burial, and there are scores of recorded acts of cannibalism.[17]

DISCRIMINATIONS

Mao and the 'Cultural Revolution Group' formed by his closest supporters (which by its coup constituted itself as the Chinese Communist Party Central Committee, CCPCC) ousted the more moderate members of the Party's ruling Politburo, including the head of China's military forces General Luo Ruiqing and the Party head in Beijing (a key position), Peng Zhen, and called on the youth of China – university and 'middle school' (high school) students – to 'Bombard the Headquarters!', meaning all those who were revisionists, 'capitalist roaders', infected by the 'Four Olds', barriers to the completion of China's revolution. Personal idolisation of Mao, and the attractiveness of educational 'reforms' which abolished exams and tests for university admission, introduced simpler curriculum materials and, very soon, suspension of classes and permission to roam the country (which most attractively of all meant free rail and bus transport to Beijing, the honeypot, to 'share revolutionary experience'), put the students into the vanguard of affairs.[18] Indeed they were officially designated as such by Mao himself, who encouraged the formation of the Red Guards, donned their armband, and – even when events began to get out of hand and provincial governments were attempting to restore order by urging students to return to classes – protected them when clashes between them and the People's Liberation Army (PLA) occurred.

At first the PLA was encouraged to join the students' activities, mainly to try to infuse them with some discipline and restraint, and to run the administration of local government which student enthusiasm and inexperience had reduced to chaos. But resulting tensions between students and soldiers, together with different Red Guard factions falling out with each other to the point of open warfare, merely deepened the anarchy.

Brandishing the recently published 'Little Red Book', ardent students leapt to Mao's call to extirpate bourgeois influences in education, the arts, and society in general. Mao himself, politically weakened by the failure of the Great Leap Forward, had come to see the government's efforts to grapple realistically with China's manifold problems as evidence of the growth of bureaucracy, perverting the meaning of the revolution. To Mao there 'appeared to be a tendency among those adopting the bourgeois capitalist road to infect and corrupt the minds of youth.'[19] Add to this his conviction that 'Whoever wants to know a thing has no way of doing so except by coming into contact with it, that is by living (practising) in its environment', and the project of reinfusing revolutionary vigour into the youth required that they 'make revolution', a key phrase.[20]

Resistance to the upsurge of student activism was at first severely criticised by the CCPCC through the medium of editorials in the press. The official line was 'Our Red Guards have performed immortal meritorious deeds in the cause of the great proletarian cultural revolution. Chairman Mao and the Central Committee of the Party enthusiastically praise their soaring revolutionary spirit, and the broad masses of workers, peasants and soldiers enthusiastically acclaim their revolutionary action', but many workers in factories and peasants on the land were annoyed by the disruption to their endeavours. They were soon admonished: the official mouthpiece of the Party, the *Renmin Ribao* (People's Daily) newspaper (RMRB), announced that the use of 'slogans to incite a number of workers and peasants to struggle against revolutionary students is extremely reactionary and completely contravenes the Party's mass line'.[21] The paper urged students to 'Sweep Away All Monsters ... criticize the old world, old ideology and culture and old customs and habits which imperialism and all exploiting classes use to poison the minds of the working people. We criticise all non-proletarian ideology, all reactionary ideology'.

In the face of attacks both verbal and physical on teachers, soon spreading to local government administrators and anyone in any official capacity, the targets of the Red Guards' activities capitulated. It was hard to do otherwise when the CCPCC published a declaration urging students 'to struggle against and crush those persons in authority who are taking the capitalist road, to criticise and repudiate the reactionary bourgeois academic "authorities" and the ideology of the bourgeoisie and all other exploiting classes and to transform education, literature and art and all other parts of the superstructure'.

The students were quick to respond to the call. A typical 'big character poster', of the kind put up at Beijing No. 2 Middle School and widely copied, addressed the teachers thus: 'You dislike from the depth of your hearts the innocent, honest, natural beauty of the broad masses of workers, peasants and soldiers. The objects of your service are the heavily made-up and gaudily dressed lords and ladies. Your souls are filthy and reactionary.'[22] This kind of rhetoric, and the actions spurred by it, spread across the country. Teachers in fear for their lives accordingly declared themselves 'pupils of the students'; their minds were a 'blank sheet' and they needed help to correct their mistakes and adhere to the revolutionary line.

Then, as productive activities, most troublingly in agriculture, began to decline sharply, the students were urged to 'unite with the broad masses of workers and peasants', which was code for going into rural areas and engaging in farmwork. This was not nearly so enticing a way of 'making revolution' and few responded unless obliged to. Shanghai became a test case; the city and its commercial and industrial operations were taken over by various factions of Red Guards, mostly at odds with each other, and rapidly descended into chaos. But their actions became a model for others across the country.

Before too long the CCPCC began to grow worried about the effects of what they had unleashed, so they tried to restrain it. The RMRB announced that 'Of late, a gust of sinister wind of struggle by force has appeared in some areas, between units and between mass organisations. It has interfered with the real orientation of the struggle, stymied the extensive democracy under the condition of democratic dictatorship, affected and wrecked production, upset the orderly process of revolution, destroyed State property, and threatened security in the lives of the people.' Red Guards were warned to guard against 'egoism' and advised to undertake 'self-rectification', and through the Third Headquarters Red Guard of Beijing the Party leadership announced that among the errors to be combatted were 'ultra-democracy and liberalism' and 'mountain stronghold mentality', the first because it led to 'subjective relaxation of pressure on the self after victory seems to be won' and both because they led to faction, sectarianism, narrow vision and the desire to preserve their own position. All were condemned as signs of 'the headquarters of the bourgeoisie in the heads of many comrades'.

The CCPCC accordingly ordered that 'exchange of revolutionary experience' – groups of students travelling around the country to join with others – must stop and everyone must return to their schools 'to participate in power seizures' and to focus on 'struggle-criticism-transformation' efforts there. The curriculum was to be restricted to 'some general knowledge' and political education. Graduates of schools and universities were to 'participate in agricultural production with contentment and participate in the great proletarian revolution in rural areas'.[23]

The role of the PLA changed. Red Guards fighting, beating people and killing them, using the excuse of revolution to settle scores and engage in looting and the destruction of property, were to be quelled by the army. Street demonstrations, disruption of transport systems, mobilisation of peasants to go to the cities, and excessive punishments were prohibited. If students 'follow a correct orientation' then even if they have made 'mistakes ... we must enthusiastically help them correct their shortcomings ... On no account should we take a side stream for the main stream, and make a fuss about the shortcomings and mistakes of the left, and refuse to give them active support.' The PLA were to have 'friendly chats' with the students, a characteristic euphemism.

The difficulty faced by the CCPCC in restoring order was exacerbated by student and graduate reluctance to accept assignment to rural areas. The CCPCC put out a circular entitled 'The Necessity for Educated Youths and Other Personnel Assigned to Work in Rural and Mountainous Areas to Persist in Staying in the Countryside to Grasp Revolution and Promote Production'. The rhetoric itself defeated its purpose; convincing youths that forking manure was the same as 'participating in the three great revolutionary movements of class struggle' and 'the construction of a new socialist countryside' was less than persuasive. An attempt to remedy a breakdown in education that was almost total in the first two years of the Cultural Revolution, 1966–8, prompted edicts stating that students must 'resume classes and make revolution' there; one such was entitled 'Stipulating Respect for Teachers and Love for Students' and emphasised the need for development of 'greater self-discipline and a relationship of political concern for and mutual help with teachers'. At the same time, teachers were to 'creatively apply Mao's thought, maintain "togetherness with the students", maintain self-discipline and have respect for the opinion of the masses.'[24] These mixed, indeed contradictory, messages – 'make revolution ... respect the teachers' – were confusing, inevitably; the 'furtherance of revolution within the universities, rather than outside them' ensured that the problems continued.

In particular, sentiment against the PLA in many Red Guard factions hardened:

> Before the Liberation the army and the people fought together to overthrow imperialism, bureaucratic capitalism, and feudalism. The relationship between army and people was like that of fish and water. After Liberation, as the target of revolution has changed from imperialism, bureaucratic capitalism and feudalism to capitalist-roaders, and as these capitalist-roaders are power-holders in the army, some of the armed forces in the revolution have not only changed their blood-and-flesh relationship with the people, but have even become tools for suppressing the revolution ... if the first great proletarian cultural revolution is to succeed, a radical change in the army will be necessary.[25]

In response Jiang Qing, Mao's wife and a leading figure of the 'Gang of Four' in the Cultural Revolution Group, wrote, 'Guided by the invincible thought of Mao Tse-tung, the revolutionary Red Guards have performed immortal exploits in the great proletarian cultural revolution. This is something no one can erase. It is our hope that you revolutionary Red Guards will guard against arrogance and rashness, carry forward your merits, overcome your shortcomings and make new contributions to the great proletarian cultural revolution.' Factionalism and intra-Red Guard strife were now blamed on 'capitalist roaders' who had infiltrated their ranks. 'As a consequence [of factionalism] the pupils were divided into revolutionary camps and both were deceived by the executors of the bourgeois reactionary line ... As the antagonism grew ... the students from the two organizations would each occupy their half of the classroom and refuse to speak to "those from the other side".'[26]

OTHERING, EXCLUDING AND CANCELLING *GROUPS*

One could go on; what is striking is not just the chaos that the Cultural Revolution quickly descended into, but the sloganising, the urging of antipathies, the labels licensing atrocities, the indiscriminate lumping together as political criminals any who did not meet the requirements of those who were utterly certain of the purity of their zeal and the rightness of their cause. In being reduced to hyperbole-slathered slogans, all discourse on matters of society and politics had been reduced to soundbites of provocation, infected by contradiction and hysteria. Perhaps among all examples in which one section of a population is whipped into a frenzy of hatred for others and the concomitant urge – put into very practical effect – to cancel them, and in which mere accusation, however indiscriminate, of being the wrong kind of person – in this case, bourgeois, revisionist, 'capitalist roader' – could go as far as murder, China's Cultural Revolution stands out.[27]

***

The persecution of the Cathars is one example of many *intra*religious cancellations. Antisemitism is an example not just of *inter*religious but racist othering, exclusion and cancellation, combined with economic resentments and political expediencies – perhaps the unholiest and least escapable mixture of hostilities ever to face any collective, worse by far in its excesses than Bosnia or Myanmar or too many other such examples, with the possible exception of one: a caste system, such as exists in India. This represents permanent exclusion of those on its bottom tier, a form of permanent cancellation, from

DISCRIMINATIONS

which there is neither escape nor relief – because whereas Jews can be and have been accepted in various places for lengthy periods of *convivencia*, or have escaped persecution by assimilation or conversion, and thus occupy a situation capable of being socially reconstructed – though at a dire cost: submitting to their own cancellation – caste is a metaphysical phenomenon, which is why escape from it is nigh impossible.

Explosions of violence and concerted actions of the kinds mentioned earlier – such as the Hutu genocide of Tutsi in Rwanda in 1994, most of the murdered 800,000 being hacked to death by machete – stand out by their vividness. But the long, slow attrition of oppression in caste systems, although also marked by episodes of individual and mob violence, is a different example of what othering, excluding and cancelling can lead to.

Caste in India is a complicated matter, not least because it has manifested in various ways in different regions of the subcontinent and different periods of its history. One of the most authoritative accounts of it, by the distinguished sociologist Professor Surinder Singh Jodhka, reveals the inadequacy of popular conceptions both of its nature and development over the three thousand years since the classification of the *varnas* – the principal divisions of society – was given in the *Rigveda*, the chief of the Vedic texts.[28] That text, and in particular the much later *Manusmriti*, dating from the first three centuries of the Common Era, in which the dharma (law) of the varnas is formalised, are the principal sources of ideas about caste, taken by the British during the Raj as a basis for their attempts to administer a hugely complex society. Just how much simplification this involved is illustrated by the fact that whereas there are four varnas, there are 3,000 castes or – not quite the same thing – 'jatis' (literally 'birth groups'), and 25,000 sub-castes, the distinctions between them based in great part on occupation. Historically the divisions were not absolute, and mobility between them was possible. On one highly plausible view, the British Raj's aim of classifying castes and jatis for census purposes did much to harden the distinctions.[29]

The *Rigveda* characterised the four varnas in terms of their origin from Brahma's body: the Brahmins, priests and teachers, from his head or mouth; the Kshatriyas, nobles and warriors, from his arms; the Vaishyas, traders and farmers, from his thighs; and the Shudras, servants, from his feet. The first three are described as 'twice-born' and the fourth 'once-born'. One's membership of a varna is a matter of one's karma. Below the four varnas, at the very lowest level of society, are the *achhoots*, 'Untouchables', this latter term outlawed in India's post-independence constitution as is the term that members of this group apply to themselves, viz. 'Dalits'; they are officially grouped as 'Scheduled Castes' (the full designation for non-varna people is 'Scheduled Castes and Scheduled Tribes') and under this label affirmative-action provisions and reservations are likewise officially made. In practice, however, Dalits continue to suffer, as they always have, from discrimination, oppression, insult, abuse, physical violence and rape – in short: persistent and wholesale othering and exclusion in all its forms.

The dividing line between the four upper castes and the Dalits is the line between 'purity' and 'pollution'. An upper caste person cannot take food from a Dalit, the latter cannot drink from the same water source, in some cases he must walk dragging a broom behind him to efface the pollution of his passing in case an upper caste person walks that way, in some places he must carry a pot on a string around his neck to spit into, if he needs to, so that he does not leave his saliva on the ground in an area where upper caste people might be present. These are just a few of the outward manifestations of the othering of Dalits, an othering that consists in profound and systematic discrimination. Jodhka writes, 'caste exhibits stark material disparities, physically segregated settlements like ghetto communities, institutionalised violence, including untouchability. Hierarchy and purity/pollution are undeniably some of the core ideas around which caste is organised. But they also produce human effects, social inequalities, economic disparities, deprivation, and violence.'[30]

And if one thought that the forces of modernity must be eroding traditional unacceptabilities like this, one would be woefully wrong; Jodhka continues:

> Caste shows no sign of disappearing in the near future. On the contrary, it appears to be far more active and agile in the early decades of the twenty-first century than perhaps ever before. Caste-based communities increasingly mobilize themselves not merely because they continue to see themselves as collective subjects, but more importantly because they perceive their collective identity of caste to be the source of their vulnerabilities *and* their strengths. Those on the lower end of the hierarchy see caste as an obstructive material reality that inhibits their

participation in the emergent structures of opportunity: in electoral politics, quality education and the corporate economy. Those on the privileged side also wish to hold onto their monopolies, often in the names of merit and modernity. Caste is thus a resource, a form of capital, whose value depends on where one is located in the traditional hierarchy, which is itself indicative of the unequal resources that caste communities possess.[31]

One of the outstanding figures in the fight to overcome the caste system was Dr Bhimrao Ramji Ambedkar, lawyer and statesman, one of the drafters of the secular constitution of India after it gained independence. The son of a soldier in the British Indian Army, he was born a Mahar – a Dalit caste – but later in life, after many decades of opposition to the caste system, he disavowed Hinduism and promoted a new casteless Buddhist movement known as Navayana. Many Dalits joined it, especially Mahars in their traditional home state of Maharashtra. Educated in the US and the UK, Ambedkar was the Justice Minister in the first government of Jawaharlal Nehru (a Brahmin) when it took power in 1947. He had already been fighting for decades for the political and civil rights of the oppressed, and continued to do so after leaving office.

Ambedkar's experience as a Dalit child was, as one would expect, highly formative. Segregated at school, Dalit children were given little attention by teachers and had to sit outside the classroom on pieces of hessian sacking that they brought to school and took home afterwards. If in need of water the

Dalit children had it poured for them from a height to prevent their impurity from somehow ascending to the pourer or the vessel. In any case the water was poured by a peon – a kind of indentured servant of the school – and if he was absent, the Dalit children stayed thirsty. This feature was the prompt for the phrase 'no peon, no water' in Ambedkar's autobiography *Waiting for a Visa*.

His luminous intellectual gifts earned Ambedkar a place at the distinguished English-medium Elphinstone High School in Bombay when his family moved there. He was the only Untouchable pupil. While there, aged fifteen, he was married in the customary arranged manner to a nine-year-old girl. From the High School he graduated to Elphinstone College, part of Bombay University; from there, after winning a scholarship from the princely state of Baroda, he went first to Columbia University in New York, coming under the influence of the philosopher John Dewey, and then to London, where he enrolled at Gray's Inn and the London School of Economics. At the end of the First World War he founded the weekly journal *Mooknayak*, 'Leader of the Silent'. It was the first of many publications promoting the Untouchables' cause. Among the early efforts of his work was organising marches of Untouchables demanding access to drinking water supplies and Hindu temples, and he publicly burned copies of the *Manusmriti* – the principal text justifying caste division – in a ceremony that his followers still re-enact every 25 December. Despite opposition from Mahatma Gandhi, who went on hunger strike to protest the move, Ambedkar succeeded in getting reserved seats in Parliament for

Untouchables, renamed 'Depressed Classes' by the British government of India in 1932. In his book *Annihilation of Caste* he rebuked Gandhi for standing in the way of improvement of the Dalits' lot; Gandhi's reason had been that reserved Parliamentary seats would divide the Hindu community.

Ambedkar is a controversial figure in India, criticised by Hindus, celebrated as *Babasaheb* ('Respected Father') by those he championed. Despite the eventual defeat of his efforts, as Jodhka's account of the continuation of the system shows, and as does (at time of writing) the determined 'Hindutva' of right-wing Indian politics, Ambedkar's long struggle is an admirable example of opposition to othering and excluding. The episodes of street activism he led are exemplary too, a chief instance being the *satyagraha* (literally 'insistence', 'holding firmly to truth', but meaning 'nonviolent resistance') he organised in the town of Nashik, in which a peaceful and orderly assembly of 15,000 marched with a military band to the Kalaram Temple to demand admission. The Brahmins of the temple barred the gates to them. 'Barring the gates' is paradigmatic exclusion; its motive lies in othering.

It is hard not to draw parallels between the position of the Jews and Dalits in history and today; or between them and racism in all its ugly forms. At the UN conference on Racism, Racial Discrimination, Xenophobia and Related Intolerance (abbreviated as 'World Conference Against Racism', WCAR) held at Durban in 2001, Dalit activists argued that caste and race are similar in the crucial respect of discrimination. Academic counter-arguments to the effect that, anthropologically, caste and race are not the same thing missed their point, which is that 'castism and racism are forms of discrimination on the basis of descent' and equally violate the rights of individuals. Impoverished communities of African Americans in US cities, and 'townships' like Soweto and Langa in South Africa, differ from such historical examples as the Jewish ghettoes of Venice and Warsaw in being the result of economic disparities and hence 'informal' in a way that ghettoes were not – although in fact the South African townships began as formal zones of exclusion too. Corralling people in a formally designated area, or making them wear badges such as the Jews' yellow star under the Nazis, are unequivocal cases of othering and exclusion. But in effect – in the effects – segregation of communities as a result of economic factors, where these are residues of historical discrimination, are no different.

***

Turn the lens of history onto the human story and one sees otherings and exclusions of whole groups and peoples everywhere, by whatever means achieved. It is against these that the battle for social justice is fought. The question is: is that battle to be won by the same means?

The counter-question that will be asked in response is what, though, of groups such as the Ku Klux Klan, and states whose population-supported governments persecute minorities or invade other countries, in many cases causing indiscriminate harm to civilian populations and even genocide? The argument of reason scarcely applies when things have gone too far, and the appeal to rights – arguing that Ku Klux Klan members have a right to their views, a majority population a right to expression of national ambitions – in short, a right to be treated according to standards they do not themselves observe – does not persuade. It is very difficult to rebut the view that when a serious line is crossed, a different argument – even that of war – is required. In this, as everywhere else in the hardest cases, the desideratum is that matters should not have been allowed to reach that pass. But they do reach that pass, very often. The dilemma is stark.

4

OTHERING, EXCLUDING AND CANCELLING *INDIVIDUALS*

Oscar Wilde was a victim of cancel culture. He was emphatically and completely cancelled by late Victorian society, which just a few years before, in 1885, had made male homosexuality a crime at law, and used the new law to brand him on the forehead with what they thought – wrongly in his case, as time has shown – was a mark of indelible infamy.

Wilde was a man of genius, and for all that he was a peacock and a deliberately provocative aesthete also, he was a man of deep social conscience, acutely critical of the hypocrisy that poisoned the society of his day. He flayed it in his plays, and in some of his short stories beautifully portrayed the nature of social compassion. When the hounds were at his heels these sentiments did nothing to protect him; instead it was the mephitic odour given off by his novel *The Picture of Dorian Gray* and his reputation as a Decadent that exposed him to their teeth.

Richard Ellmann, in his masterly and detailed biography of Wilde, recounts the first meeting between his subject and

'Bosie', Lord Alfred Douglas, who proved to be the cause of Wilde's downfall.[1] The meeting was, in itself, unremarkable and brief. A mutual friend brought Bosie to Wilde's Tite Street home near Tedworth Square in London's Chelsea, and Wilde, at that time engaged in doting on another young man, did not immediately fall in love. The description of Bosie as 'blond with a pale alabaster face', slender and short, thought 'charming' by his friends, precedes Ellmann's judgement on him, which falls like a gavel in the next line: Bosie was 'in temperament totally spoiled, reckless, insolent and, when thwarted, fiercely vindictive'. Wilde saw only Bosie's beauty, and gave him a deluxe edition of *Dorian Gray*. When he learned that the young man was studying classics at Oxford, he offered himself as a supplementary tutor.

That was in 1891. By the following summer Wilde was thoroughly besotted. To his friend Robbie Ross he wrote that Bosie 'is quite like a narcissus – so white and gold ... he lies like a hyacinth on the sofa, and I worship him'. But Bosie quickly became a drain both on Wilde and on Wilde's purse. Ellmann says that his letters to Bosie combined 'declarations of financial embarrassment and deepening love'. Wilde soon realised that Bosie's recklessness was ungovernable. The youth had a wild temper; Wilde's infatuated praises of his poems gave him an unwarranted belief in his own talent, and he demanded that Wilde treat him as his equal in art, flying into a rage at any suggestion otherwise. He especially made free with Wilde's money in the joint escapades they took with increasing abandon into London's gay underground. It was in that wilderness, made dark and unsavoury by the prejudices of the day, that the prosecution lawyers in Wilde's indecency trial found witnesses to testify against him. Even before then Wilde was blackmailed by at least one of them, the lad in question using letters Wilde had carelessly left in the pocket of a jacket he had given him.

Bosie dragged Wilde down with many tentacles. It was not just himself as the object of Wilde's devotion but, through it, the situations he got Wilde into. The chief of these was Bosie's toxic relationship with his father, the Marquess of Queensberry, a man in his own different way as tumultuous and ungovernable as his son. Wilde was crushed in the collision between them. Bosie induced Wilde to sue his father over the latter's allegations about Wilde. Wilde – knight errant charging unthinkingly into battle for his beloved in distress – lost the case, and was arrested for the indecency Queensberry charged him with.

Queensberry, reputedly a vicious man who was divorced by his first wife for adultery and abandoned by his second wife after a year of marriage because of his brutality, was outraged when he learned that his son was in a homosexual relationship with Wilde. He left a card for Wilde inscribed 'For Oscar Wilde, posing Somdomite' (his spelling was no better than his character). At Bosie's instigation Wilde sued Queensberry for libel. The Marquess's barrister, the celebrated Sir Edward Carson, decided to portray Wilde as a degenerate older man who seduced youths, and found a number of the rent boys of Piccadilly Circus ('Pick-a-willy Circus' in the jargon of the day) prepared to testify to that effect for a monetary consideration. As it happens, these boys were indeed regular clients of Wilde and Bosie, who had redirected their sexual activities from each other to this shared source. The unsavoury character of this fact has not diminished in the time since; but such is human nature, not even at its worst. Clearly on a losing wicket, Wilde dropped his case. Queensberry countersued for costs, and bankrupted Wilde. And then he sent the evidence collected by Carson to the police, who arrested Wilde, and charged him with gross indecency under the new law.

Wilde was convicted and sentenced to two years' hard labour. When released in 1897 he went straight into exile in France, and died, broken as much in health as reputation, three years later – as it happens, in a tawdry hotel less than a hundred metres from where these words were written, No. 13 Rue des Beaux Arts in Paris's sixth *arrondissement*. His funeral was conducted in the Church of Saint-Germain-des-Pres in December 1900, with no more than a dozen people present. Among them were his faithful friend Robbie Ross and his destroyer Bosie. A twist to the tale is that two of Bosie's ancestors are buried in that church. Wilde's body was taken from there to its first temporary resting place, in the Bagneux cemetery, deposited in a short-lease grave and covered with quicklime to scour the flesh from the bones. Nine years later his skeleton was transferred to Pierre Lachaise cemetery where, a few years later again, the Epstein monument to him was 'arrested' by the Paris police because its display of genitals offended their sense of what is fitting in a mortuary setting – an untypical quirk for the French.

Wilde had clarity, a superlative gift, which enabled him to cut through hypocrisy and anatomise human motivation in his plays, and to catch the demon at work that drove Dorian Gray's vanity and hubris. Vanity and hubris: Wilde had plenty of both, but though the former was excusable in one who placed value on the aesthetic dimensions of life, the latter should have rung alarm bells for him. The fatal acts of bravado that led him to sue Bosie's father were hubristic in the extreme. He had far more than enough clarity to see the danger, yet plunged into it.

Acknowledging Wilde's failings, the point remains that what happened to him was a paradigm case of cancellation. No matter that he had served the prison term decreed by law, and thus 'paid his debt to society'; society would not be satiated by so meagre a punishment. Nothing less than complete cancellation would do – a life sentence by annihilation of reputation and expulsion from their midst. Because the stain of a father's sins blights his progeny, his sons Cyril and Vyvyan changed their surname to Holland; their Wilde name, now illustrious in the history of literature, was cancelled too.

It is possible that at least some of those who sin by today's current lights are in the same case. The net flung over miscreants has a very close mesh, dragging in small as well as big fish by the metric of sin. The word 'indiscriminate' forces itself on conscience, or should.

***

Another case of individual cancelling, this time in its extreme form, is the story of Michael Servetus. Once again, seeing what was at stake – pun intended – is illustrative of how tragedy attends entrenched positions that make mutual comprehension impossible.[2]

To understand Servetus's story it is necessary to understand the theologian John Calvin, whose austere and unforgiving doctrines of predestination and eternal damnation constituted a version of Christianity that permitted no dissent. Among all who were adamant in their condemnation of heresy – in Calvin's case meaning disagreement with his views – he was an outstanding example. Those views were expounded in his chief work, *The Institutes of the Christian Religion*, standardly referred to as the *Institutio*. In his commentary on Deuteronomy, chapter 13, which enjoins stoning to death 'false prophets' and 'dreamers of dreams', Calvin wrote:

> This law might at first appear too severe. Why should anyone be punished thus for merely having spoken? But if anyone slanders a mortal man he is punished; shall we allow a blasphemer of the living God to go unpunished? If a mortal prince suffers injury, death scarcely seems sufficient revenge for it. Yet when the sovereign emperor God is reviled by a word, is nothing to be done? God's glory and our salvation are so intertwined that a traitor to God is also an enemy of humanity, and worse than a murderer because he leads poor souls to damnation. Some say that because the crime consists only of words there is no cause for such severe punishment. But we muzzle barking dogs; shall we leave men free to open their mouths and say what they please? ... God makes it plain that the false prophet is to be stoned without mercy. We are to crush beneath our heels all

natural affections when His honour is at stake. The father should not spare his child, nor one brother another, nor the husband his wife, nor the friend that friend who is dearer to him than life.

The deity was even happy to see the killing of Amalekite babies, Calvin pointed out (though, he added, 'we must rest assured that God would suffer only those infants to be destroyed whom he had already damned and destined to eternal death'); therefore we must not hesitate to destroy likewise any who impugn God's honour. Humans must not presume to be more compassionate than the deity, for heretics and blasphemers 'are worse than brigands who cut the throat of a wayfarer'.[3]

Servetus was a victim of these inexorable views. A Spaniard, he grew up in the Spanish Netherlands, a speaker of Flemish who had been educated by admirers of the undogmatic, fair-minded humanist Erasmus. He served on the staff of the confessor of King Charles I of Spain (grandson of the 'Catholic Monarchs' Isabella and Ferdinand). This confessor, by name Quintana, had for a time been attracted by Luther's teachings, but had decided not to leave the Church. At the outset Servetus was even more orthodox than Quintana; his brother was a Catholic priest and his mother a benefactor of the Church. But the subtly mounting influence of Erasmus and Quintana had their effect. Servetus became interested in the mystical movement known as 'Illuminism' among *conversos* (converted Jews) in Spain, and while studying law at Toulouse University he began to ponder why those Jews and Muslims who had refused to convert during Torquemada's time had chosen not to do so.

How, he asked himself, could they not accept the truth taught by the Church, that God had revealed himself in Christ for the redemption of humankind?

Servetus concluded that the stumbling block was the monotheism central to Jewish and Muslim belief, which entailed rejection of Christianity's doctrine of the Trinity. He saw that to Jews and Muslims this doctrine amounted to tritheism, graphically represented in paintings and statuary that portrayed Father, Son and Holy Ghost as separate entities – respectively an old bearded man, a crucified young man, and a dove or flame or beam of light. At Toulouse University Servetus found himself among enthusiasts avidly studying Scripture and debating the absence from it of a number of central Church doctrines, not least that of the Trinity. The Gospels mentioned the three persons as separate beings; it was the Council of Nicaea in 325 CE that had decided, in order to combat the Arian heresy whose central tenet was the separateness of the persons, that the Father and the Son are 'consubstantial' (of one substance; the same thing) and that the Holy Ghost 'proceeds' from them, 'proceeds' being one of those many characteristically meaningless terms that blanket theological fudges.

Servetus could not see why Jews and Moors should be denied God's grace on the basis of a doctrine that had no scriptural basis. He examined the development of Trinitarian doctrine in the explanations provided by St Augustine and St Thomas Aquinas, which relied on analogies, and the proofs attempted by Richard of St Victor in his argument that God is love and love requires at least two persons (the lover and the beloved), and to be perfect a third (so that jealousy is possible though not experienced). Most others argued that the Trinity is a mystery that can be neither explained nor understood, only believed ('mystery' being theology's last resort).

None of this satisfied Servetus, understandably enough, so he rejected the doctrine of the Trinity, arguing that Jesus was a human man whom God had joined with the eternal divine Word to create an 'incarnate Christ'. From the viewpoint of orthodoxy there were two unacceptable aspects to this; not just denial of the Trinity itself but the idea that humanity can be divine, 'the mingling of God with man' as Servetus put it. The idea that man can be elevated to divine status was a Renaissance trope. Calvin saw it as the opposite: the lowering of God to human status. His trenchant views about 'protecting the honour of God' could not tolerate such a thing.

Servetus published his views in a book called *On the Errors of the Trinity*. Because the Erasmian influence at the Spanish court had dissipated – the Holy Office by then had put Erasmus's works on the Index of Forbidden Books – Servetus thought it politic to move first to Strasbourg and then another Protestant city, Basel, where Erasmus was buried and his liberal influence lingered. Yet even there Servetus's views found no favour. He sent his book to Quintana and certain other theologians including Melanchthon; all denounced him. One of them, the Bishop of Saragossa, encouraged the Inquisition to extradite him to Spain for trial. He was now a fugitive. He changed his name to Michael Villeneuve and went to Lyon, finding a job as an editor and proofreader in the relatively new industry of printed-books publishing. But he could not restrain himself. In an edition he prepared of the Bible he added a preface saying that the Old Testament prophets were not foretelling Christ's coming but only adverting to their own times. In an edition of Ptolemy's geography he quoted a remark to the effect that Palestine 'was not a land of great promise', later held against him as impugning the endeavours of Moses.

When editing lost its savour Servetus went to Paris and studied anatomy with Vesalius, qualified as a doctor, and returned to Lyon to practise medicine, which he did for twelve years. He might have lived out his life usefully and peacefully in this way, free of the danger of his Unitarian views. But he could not leave theology alone. He set about calculating the date of the Parousia – the Second Coming – and worked out that it was soon, in 1585, thus within his own lifetime. He added his studies in mysticism, Neoplatonism and the doctrines of Hermes Trismegistus to conclude that the trope of Christ as 'Light of the World' was literal: Christ glowed in the heart of gems, in the sun and moon, in the sparkling surface of rivers and ponds. Excited, he decided to try to persuade Calvin that it was wrong to think as Calvin did, that Christ is transcendent, wholly beyond the world, diametrically opposite to the idea of his being present in it as glitters and sparks. Drawn as a moth to a flame – quite literally, as it proved – by Calvin's great celebrity, wishing to test his views against those of the most famous religious figure of the day, Servetus sent Calvin his book, and did not bother to conceal his identity.

Calvin, without commenting on Servetus's views, merely sent him a copy of his *Institutio* by way of reply, to put him right. Irritated, Servetus scribbled insulting annotations in the *Institutio*'s margins and returned it to Calvin, together with a document he punningly entitled *Restitutio*. Calvin remarked to a friend that if Servetus ever came to Geneva, he would not leave it alive.

These exchanges happened in 1546. Matters might have ended there, but Servetus would not have been Servetus if they had. He reworked his *Restitutio* and published it at Lyon in 1553. He had grown more acerbic with time, and the extended book was an intemperate affair; he likened the Trinity to the three-headed guard dog of Hades, Cerberus. It did not take long for him to be identified. Calvin collaborated with the Catholic Inquisition to have him stopped; despite the bitter differences between Calvinism and Catholicism, a cause of this kind was sufficient to get these unlikely collaborators into bed together. Servetus was arrested by the Inquisition in Lyon, but escaped from prison. He was found guilty *in absentia* and his effigy was strangled and burned, along with every copy of the *Restitutio* that could be found (only three are known today).

And then, amazingly, stupidly, Servetus went to Geneva. Or perhaps it was not amazing and stupid; one theory has it that Servetus was in league with a group there seeking to overthrow Calvin. But in any case Geneva's city fathers were as unfriendly to heresy as Calvin himself, so when Servetus was recognised, as he almost immediately was, he was arrested and put on trial. Every one of his crimes was itemised, from the remark about Palestine to the major heresy about the Trinity and the nature of Jesus. Servetus said that Calvin's emphasis on original sin and predestination made man no better than a stone, bereft of freedom and agency, while Calvin said that Servetus's doctrine of humanity's participation in the divine insulted God because it made Him subject to the flesh's failings. The battle of views between them figuratively reprised the contrast between the humanistic optimism of the Renaissance and the Reformation's most severe version of fundamentalism.

Servetus behaved badly during his trial, insulting Calvin and demanding that the judges put Calvin on trial instead, and give him, Servetus, Calvin's property in compensation. The court denied him a defence lawyer. He was alone, frightened, soon in rags, and tormented by lice in his prison cell. When the Inquisition in France requested that he be handed to them for trial he begged the Genevan court not to agree, but to finish with him there. This they did, after consulting the other Protestant cities of Switzerland, which advised severity but not the death penalty. The judges of Geneva were, however, resolved on the death penalty:

> We syndics, judges of criminal cases in this city, having witnessed the trial conducted before us at the instance of our lieutenant against you, Michel Servet de Villeneufve of Aragon in Spain, and having witnessed your confessions and writings, judge that you, Servetus, have for long promulgated false and thoroughly heretical doctrines, despising all remonstrance and correction, and have with malice, perversity and obstinacy spread even in printed books opinions against God the Father, the Son, and the Holy Ghost, in a word against the fundamentals of the Christian

religion, and that you have tried to make schism and trouble in the Church of God by which many souls might have been ruined and lost, a thing horrible, shocking, scandalous and infectious. And you have had neither shame nor horror of setting yourself against the Divine Majesty and Holy Trinity, and have obstinately tried to infect the world with your stinking heretical poison ... we sentence and condemn you, Michael Servetus, to be bound and taken to Champel and there attached to a stake and burned with your books to ashes.[4]

Servetus had not been expecting the death penalty. Terrified, he pleaded for pity; from his cell he sent for Calvin and begged his forgiveness. Calvin coldly said he should seek it instead from God. When he was taken to the stake Servetus was accompanied by the man who had brought Calvin to Geneva in the first place, William Farel. Farel tried to persuade him to renounce his errors, but Servetus remained silent. His book was tied to him, and the flames were lit. He was heard to pray, 'Have pity on me Jesus thou son of the eternal God.' Farel remarked that if he had moved the adjective – 'Have pity on me Jesus thou eternal son of God' – he might have been saved.

From the viewpoint of those who sincerely believed in the doctrines of their faith, Servetus represented a danger, a serious danger: 'many souls might have been ruined and lost, a thing horrible, shocking, scandalous and infectious'. They meant it; they were devout, they were shocked, scandalised and afraid of what such infection might do to immortal souls for all eternity. From his own viewpoint Servetus cleaved more strictly to Scripture itself, in one direction, and in the

OTHERING, EXCLUDING AND CANCELLING *INDIVIDUALS*

other to the application of reason, applying literally what the Scriptures proposed: 'Jesus as the light of the world'. Why could not others see what he saw, he thought? That he was an intemperate man who made matters worse by ill-judging the way to make his case does not obscure the fact that he was intelligent and equally committed. His enthusiasm and frustration combined to make him a victim of what he opposed; a striking illustration of how this combination can, and all too often does, result in self-defeat. A parallel can be drawn with more activist proponents of any cause, however just.

In the case of such murderous theological disputes a third-party observer would likely argue that both sides were reasoning from false premises. That they reasoned with cogency from these false premises does not excuse them. What made matters worse is that both sides jointly accepted at least some of the key false premises. Yet in the circumstances there could be no common ground to the endpoints that their divergent inferences reached. And, having both accepted some of the key premises, they then jointly abandoned what Erasmus had urged; that the question of who was right and who was wrong in theology should be left up to the deity in whom both sides believed.

This Erasmian solution is, however, appropriate only to theology. When it comes to racism and sexism, to all unjustified discrimination and its otherings and exclusions, there is no posthumous resolution; the rights at issue are a matter too present, too insistent, for kicking into touch. Where and what, then, is the solution, if justice is to be achieved justly? That is the question.

***

DISCRIMINATIONS

There is a striking literary exploration of cancellation in the story of Hester Prynne in Hawthorne's *The Scarlet Letter*. The description of the grim and inflexibly self-righteous crowd outside the Boston prison on the day Hester Prynne left it, her baby daughter Pearl in her arms and the flaming scarlet letter 'A' on her breast, is a description of every merciless crowd of self-righteous cancellers everywhere, when cancellers are at their worst short of murder. The women in the crowd thought that instead of a stitched-on patch of shame, Hester should have been branded on the forehead with a searing iron. Sexual crime – in Hester's case a baby out of wedlock, connoting fornication, adultery, sexual congress outside the strict confines of sacredly licensed marriage – was beyond the pale for the Puritans of early Boston.

Sex as a concern of special moral anxiety is a peculiarly Christian thing. The Old Testament condemns 'unnatural sex' but not sex; none of the other major civilisations had the hostility to things of the body that Christianity adopted from the philosophies that divided what is material from what is mental or spiritual.[5] The sculptors of Khajuraho in India, the *shunga* ('Spring Pictures') of Japanese erotic art, China's *chungonghua*, display no such disgust. King Solomon, Turkish pashas, Chinese mandarins, had their numerous harems; it is claimed by some – contested by others – that in all societies from the Sumerians to the Romans temple prostitution was a feature; the unequivocal evidence of Pompeii's murals, conjoined with the lack of any outrage about its allure as a holiday destination in the early Roman Empire, is evidence of more relaxed attitudes than became the norm when ideas about the body as a site of sin, filth, degradation, devil's bait, danger, took up a large tract of Christian moral thinking. This thinking was not motivated by concern for women and girls helplessly subjected to treatment as utensils for male sexual satisfaction and procreation; on the contrary, females were condemned for being attractive for these purposes, blamed for leading males astray. On getting down to the most unadorned facts of the matter, one sees that the alternative to what was in effect a form of sexual slavery for women was what was in effect a form of imprisonment – specifically, imprisonment in the domestic sphere. Not much of a choice.

It is noteworthy, in this connection, that there is a difference between the liberation struggles of women and gay men over sex. Gay men have had to battle a history-long oppression of attitudes stemming from Leviticus, chapter 20, whose proscriptions survived into Islam too. Women have battled a different enemy: biology. The relatively costless and relatively indiscriminate urge for sexual satisfaction on the part of males, which prompts them to behaviour that is (again putting matters bluntly) predatory, contrasts sharply with the potentially high cost to females of sexual encounters – pregnancy, childbirth, motherhood – even leaving aside, which one should not, the decided objections women have to engaging in sex with anyone not of their choice. In the effort to control male behaviour in this respect, so long given too much licence by social frameworks in which predatory behaviour was in practice condoned and in its own circles applauded, the Me Too movement figures as a flagship. The key issue is consent; and that is precisely as it should be. Ethological studies show that sexual coercion of females by males is widespread in nature; the formerly held belief that non-human mating universally proceeds only at female invitation and selection is incorrect.[6] If there were a mark of 'civilisation' as this term is used to denote a state of affairs where rights and interests are given their due, the respect agenda is it.

That Hawthorne's Hester Prynne embroidered her 'A' so beautifully, that she walked from the prison with such quiet dignity, affronted the assembled spectators. Made to stand for three hours on the scaffold exposed to the condemnation of the crowd, she refused to name her child's father, though the name was demanded from her as she stood there. 'The unhappy culprit sustained herself as best a woman might, under the heavy weight of a thousand unrelenting eyes, all fastened upon her, and concentrated at her bosom', Hawthorne writes:

> It was almost intolerable to be borne. Of an impulsive and passionate nature, she had fortified herself to encounter the stings and venomous stabs of public contumely, wreaking itself in every variety of insult; but there was a quality so much more terrible in the solemn mood of the popular mind, that she longed rather to behold all those rigid countenances contorted with scornful merriment, and herself the object. Had a roar of laughter burst from the multitude – each man, each woman, each little shrill-voiced child, contributing their individual parts – Hester Prynne might have repaid them all with a bitter and disdainful smile. But, under the leaden infliction which it was her doom to endure, she felt, at moments, as if she must needs

shriek out with the full power of her lungs, and cast herself from the scaffold down upon the ground, or else go mad at once.

Until she left for England years later, Hester lived in a secluded cottage on the edge of the settlement, eking a living from her exquisite needlework. The novel is as much about her formerly long-lost husband Chillingworth and, more especially, the minister Arthur Dimmesdale (who turns out to be Pearl's father), and questions of guilt, sin, reparation, and emblematically the allusion to the first-ever-recorded cancellation – the expulsion of Adam and Eve from Eden – as about Hester herself. But it offers a powerful picture of the experience of the cancelled individual. When Hester returns to Boston and later dies, she is buried close to Dimmesdale's grave, and her tombstone has on it a depiction of her badge, no longer a badge of shame but of triumph.

No doubt most of those cancelled by social media 'pile-ons' in the tumult of the present's culture wars, whether deserving of opprobrium or unfairly condemned, feel that they are victims. Their own accounts of victimhood, independently of whether there was substance in the attack on them, often look like special pleading, apt to strike at least some as distasteful and untrustworthy. The same does not apply to e.g. Holocaust survivors and asylum-seekers fleeing documented persecution in their homelands; truth here is not alloyed by opinion. It takes literature to make the case for those who, if they venture a defence on their own account, thereby invite a dilution of it by the suspicion that lingers in the minds of hearers. That, indeed, is one of the chief effects of trial by social media: flung mud sticks. But in a literary depiction such as Hawthorne gives, the suffering of the condemned involves no special pleading. It is brought before the reader as it were documentarily.

Of course, in non-fictional circumstances, the case made by a victim or self-proclaimed victim has to be justified, and that is the problem. Flung mud is all of one colour. To bracket the would-be Lothario with the sex pest and both with the actual rapist, consigning them to the same silo, is an obvious mistake, but it is not just vehement misandry that commits it. The rapist needs to be in prison, but the would-be Lothario and the sex pest need education, preferably well before they become either.[7] The difference between a sewn-on patch that can be unstitched at some point, and a searing-iron brand on a forehead, lies in the degree of irreversibility. The question, another version of the question asked earlier, is how, at this point in the renegotiation of relations between the sexes – *pace* adherence to a classification that leaves aside recognition of the non-binary nature of gender and sexuality – this is to be achieved. Anger blurs distinctions; the Aristotle Principle is forgotten here. Whose rights, what wrongs, are at issue? How are the latter to be calibrated, and how addressed?

If Hester had identified Dimmesdale as Pearl's father while on the scaffold, he too would have been cancelled by the Puritan community, and immediately excluded. But it is unlikely that he would have been imprisoned, as Hester was, or like her made to wear a mark of shame. The double standard is doubtless far older than Genesis, but it is in this latter text that the first, most unashamed version of it is recorded

OTHERING, EXCLUDING AND CANCELLING *INDIVIDUALS*

– in the story of Judah and Tamar (Genesis, chapter 38), in which a would-be canceller is 'called out' but for the wrong thing.

The story is that the girl Tamar married the eldest son, named Er, of the patriarch Judah – a son of Jacob and founder of the tribe that bears his name. But Er was 'wicked in the Lord's sight, so the Lord put him to death' before he could have a child. As custom demanded, Judah gave Tamar his second son Onan as a husband, for Onan's duty was 'to raise up seed' to his brother's name. But Onan did not wish to do this, and instead of impregnating Tamar he 'spilled his seed on the ground'. The Lord struck him dead for this crime, and therefore somehow masturbation (rather than Onan's *coitus interruptus*) became a sin for the next three thousand years.[8]

Rendered anxious by the fatal effect that Tamar appeared to have on his sons, Judah hesitated to marry her to his third son, Shelah, as custom demanded; and he delayed so long that Tamar eventually took action. She disguised herself as a prostitute and waited for Judah on the road from the village. He saw her and 'went in unto her' as biblical phraseology has it. When he asked her what she wanted as payment, she said, 'A kid from your flock' – an excellent way of putting it. And as surety she demanded his staff, bracelets and ring. Back at his camp Judah told his men that he had been with a harlot and they must take the payment to her, but when the men took a baby goat to the road there was no one there.

Three months later Tamar was denounced before Judah 'for having played the harlot, and behold, she is with child by whoredom'. Judah said, 'Bring her forth, and let her be burnt'

– or as we might now say, cancelled completely. Tamar produced the tokens she had demanded of Judah and reproached him for denying her Shelah; 'And Judah acknowledged [the tokens], and said, She hath been more righteous than I'.

Though it does Judah credit for confessing to his failing in the matter of custom, he does not blink an eye, nor does anyone else, at the double standard so shriekingly manifested by the tale: whereas he can consort with a harlot by the wayside and speak freely of it to his followers, she must be burned to death. Little changed as regards the double standard until recently, if indeed it really has changed. In such matters the dice are loaded as to which party will suffer cancellation by opprobrium, punishment and rejection – or in Tamar's case and that of so many millions of others, death. A 'fallen woman' was long excluded from 'good' society; in circumstances where there were few options for a woman to survive, either the nunnery – if it would have her – or more likely the streets beckoned. Society othered, excluded and thereby cancelled women who did not conform to its standards. *The Scarlet Letter* is a portrait of one paradigmatic such.

Connecting the double standard to cancelling should stir at least some consciences. There is, after all, another text that invites stone-throwing only from the sinless. But this offers an invitation in its turn; impugning a smoker who tells another person that he should not smoke on the grounds that the adviser is himself a smoker, is to attack the arguer not the argument – an instance of the *ad hominem* fallacy. A sinner might condemn a sin in this kind of case, though in many

OTHERING, EXCLUDING AND CANCELLING *INDIVIDUALS*

other cases the charge of hypocrisy is justified, as when a cocaine-sniffing politician votes to criminalise cocaine use in order to punish others. Distinguishing between the cases where a plea of *experto crede* ('believe one who knows') is justified and where hypocrisy is in play can sometimes take thought.

Neither of these considerations gets to the heart of contemporary cancel culture, however. Consider cases where cancelling activism has a compelling motivation: one such is the 'Dilbert' example. In 2023 Scott Adams, the creator of the Dilbert comic strip (which, since its first appearance in 1989, tellingly and popularly satirised work culture and was syndicated in over 2,000 newspapers), posted a profanity-larded outburst on YouTube in which among other things Adams described African Americans as a 'hate group' and advised 'white people' to 'get the hell away from black people; just get the fuck away'.[9] In consequence Dilbert and his creator were cancelled; the cartoon was dropped from almost all newspapers, and Adams's book deal was withdrawn by a publisher. The unacceptability of racism explains and justifies the anger; the question is whether, to invoke Gilbert and Sullivan's Lord High Executioner, the punishment fits the crime, given that it appears so different in individual and corporate instances. Compare Adams's fate with that of the Heineken and Dove companies. In 2018 Heineken introduced a new light beer, and ran an advertisement in which a glass of beer is slid along a bar-top, passing several darker-skinned customers and arriving at a lighter-skinned one, with the slogan 'lighter is better'. In 2017 Dove advertised a body-wash as having excellent dirt-removing properties, and ran an advertisement in which an African American woman removes her shirt and is instantly transformed into a white woman because she has used Dove body-wash. Both Heineken and Dove apologised and removed the advertisements – and continued to trade profitably.

Racism is an evil, and the campaign against it is unequivocally justified. That includes the unconscious, or conscious but masked, forms of racism that were perceived in the advertisements cited. The idea that one cannot change racists by persuasion and education underlies the idea – perhaps the instinct – that they should be denied a voice, and thus prevented from infecting others with their attitudes, and stopped from causing problems for the targets of their prejudice. By displaying intolerance of intolerance, others might be persuaded to check their own propensities to intolerance. Perhaps the belief is that collateral damage is acceptable in the struggle. It seems to fall most heavily on individuals, stripping them of reputation and income. As already mentioned, apology and a promise of reform seem to carry little weight. Individuals financially well-protected from the effects of cancelling can ride out the consequences of loss of reputation, though not the loss of reputation itself; Kanye West, who made antisemitic comments, expressing admiration for Hitler and denial of the Holocaust, is cited as an example, for despite the withdrawal of his deals with the brands Gap, Adidas, Balenciaga and others, he remained wealthy according to Forbes, despite its claim that his fortune dropped from $1.8 billion to $400 million as a result of the outcries prompted by his statements.[10] But individuals whose livelihoods disappear with their reputations make the question about the proportionality of the punishment more pressing. Does the 'acceptable collateral damage' argument apply to individuals without qualification?

This is a hard question, because the stakes are high in the battle, which without question must be won, to overcome racism and sexism. Public outcry through social media presents a difficulty because it is trial without due process or appeal, and there is no guarantee that – in less clear-cut cases than those just cited – the same unequivocally applies to real-life Hester Prynnes, as individuals, when the assumption of irredeemability is applied.

Evidently, the crux of the matter is rights and how decisions about right and wrong affect them. That is the topic of the next chapter.

5

RIGHT(S) AND WRONG(S)

Dealing with the complexities raised in the preceding chapters requires clarity about what underlies them and is at stake in them. This involves getting into the details of some further significant concepts, as outlined below.

Everything now to be said turns on a crucial distinction, which – before noting some qualifications – can be put in binary terms as follows: individuals have *rights, obligations* and *interests*; groups have *interests*. A chief interest of a group is the rights and interests of its individual members, but the group itself does not have rights. This claim is controversial, not just in social activist contexts but as a result of interpretations of UN conventions of rights; see below. An important corollary of this point concerns *identity*. Individuals have multiple identities in the sense that they can and typically do belong to a number of groups, but *qua* individuals they have a determinate identity as *that entity*, whereas groups have indeterminate identities in the sense that their boundaries and memberships are fuzzy.[1] The relationship between individuals and groups illustrates this; individuals can claim or seek membership of a group, a group can deny membership to an individual or can claim an individual as a member – and can claim that an individual is a member of another group – which, in regard to these latter two cases, the individual may respectively refuse or deny. An individual may disclaim being J. Bloggs of Acacia Villas (for example upon being arrested by the police) but various considerations will generally determine that he is indeed that individual, whereas a group might refuse to accept an individual's claim to belong to it on the grounds e.g. that he is undesirable, or a Pretendian, that is, is one whom the group respectively does not wish to include or does not recognise as one of its own.

These remarks constitute a first pass at the issues; they contain a welter of complexities. First consider the concept of an 'individual'. A human being is an individual, a company like Amazon is an individual, a state like France is an individual; these two latter are corporate individuals. The majority of human individuals are *persons* in the forensic – that is, legal and moral – sense in having both rights and obligations, and with them the competencies to make autonomous decisions about aspects of their lives and activities, and to do such things as own property, enter into contracts, and the like. On this concept of personhood, companies, clubs, universities and states are also persons: they have rights and obligations.

A human individual is a person in the full sense of the term when in possession of rational faculties of mind, which means that babies and people with psychoses or dementia are therefore not persons in the forensic sense; they are accorded personhood by courtesy of the fact that they will be or were persons, and have rights (as do non-human animals), but are not said to have obligations or duties correlative to those rights, such as – importantly – respecting the rights of others.

One of the features of 'group identity' considerations, which have become a major matter over the course of the period since the formalisation of human rights instruments after 1945, is the variety of groups and definitions of groups that are at issue in the claim that, contrary to the assertion in the first paragraph above, groups indeed have rights. The relationship between possession of rights and determinacy of identity is the point at issue here. If the criteria for membership of a group are clear-cut – there is something that settles completely whether one is a member of the group or not – does that not give the group itself a clear-cut identity and therefore the status of personhood (*qua* possession of rights and obligations)? What appear to be focal cases of groups with clear-cut membership criteria are clubs, companies, universities and states – but these are already persons, corporate persons, by the definition of personhood: bearers of rights and responsibilities. Are there groups that are not persons in this sense but have clear-cut membership criteria?

One suggestion is the Jewish community. On more strict definitions of what it is to be Jewish, all and only those with a Jewish mother are so. That is a clear-cut criterion. But most Jewish denominations accept converts who do not have Jewish mothers, providing they will sincerely accept to live by the Jewish commandments and (if male) be circumcised. But note that because anyone born of a Jewish mother can automatically be granted Israeli citizenship, the implication is that the state of Israel regards the worldwide Jewish community as, in effect, a forensic person, with all that this entails. Because at time of writing there are an estimated 15.7 million Jews in the world, just 0.2% of the world population, Israel's openness to granting citizenship to them does not represent a burden to it – rather the contrary; half of them already live in Israel[2] – and is unique in a world where migration and asylum-seeking are regarded as a major and generally unwelcome problem.

But to say that 'world Jewry' has a right – to citizenship of Israel – is shorthand for saying that each member of this group has that right. It is a trick of semantics to apply a property of individual members of a group to the group as a whole; in fact it is a fallacy, known as the 'fallacy of composition', illustrated by pointing out the error in saying that because each member of a pod of whales is a whale, the pod is a whale. This fallacy is at work in the concept of 'group rights'. Contention arises when discussion of 'national self-determination' is at issue, and ethnic groups such as the Rohingya in Myanmar are persecuted, the Rohingya not constituting a corporate nation state; yet it seems natural, and is indeed correct, to speak of the rights of the Rohingya. But note the give-away point: we say 'the Rohingya *have* rights' (they most certainly do) and not 'the Rohingya *has* rights'. Rohingya individuals are persecuted because they belong to the group constituted by Rohingya individuals, and there are criteria for allocating individuals to that group; but the existence of such criteria does not confer corporate personhood on the group.

DISCRIMINATIONS

The essential point – that rights pertain to individuals, whether human (and non-human animal) or corporate – matters for much that is at stake in the struggles against violations of rights in our world.

The concepts of 'race' and 'ethnicity' come immediately into view. 'Ethnicity' denotes cultural and linguistic affinities while 'race' is a more complicated and much-contested notion, originally turning on the idea that humankind consists of distinct groups separated by inherited physical differences outwardly manifested by skin colour, stature, hair texture and facial features. But this idea has been shown by genetic studies to have no biological validity.[3] It is no accident that the concept of race emerged in the seventeenth and eighteenth centuries CE as the globalising expansion of Europe solidified into colonisations, the concept predicated wholly on physical appearance combined, to a lesser extent, with cultural factors (a lesser extent because physically similar peoples engaged in different cultural practices in different places).

Despite the conclusive genetic evidence, the category of race persists in some official forms – the US's Office of Management and Budget (OMB) Standards lists five 'racial categories' on its website (American Indian or Alaska Native, Asian, Black or African American, Native Hawaiian or Other Pacific Islander, White)[4] – and it most certainly continues to exist in *racism*. In the case of the OMB classification the motivation derives from the National Institutes of Health's 'Human Subjects System' in which reports of clinical trials data have to be sensitive to the fact that different groups of people have varying health susceptibilities – for example, people in the third category listed above have a higher risk of hypertension-related disease. Confusingly from the point of view of the lack of biogenetic differences of 'race', some of these susceptibility differences are inherited – sickle cell anaemia is more prevalent in African populations, thought to be an evolutionary adaptation protective against malaria – while other differences are functions of lifestyle including diet, thus involving ethnic factors. The OMB/NIH use of 'racial categories' relates to these considerations. It could be argued that better collective designations might be chosen.

The clincher as regards the quite different matter of *racism* – discriminatory attitudes based chiefly on differences of physical appearance and, to a lesser extent, culture traditionally associated with them – is that there are no moral, legal, political or social grounds (these overlap) for treating any human beings differently from other human beings except when doing so affirmatively respects the needs and interests of some relative to others (for two examples: separating toilet facilities for men and women – though now a point of contention in some contexts – and making provision for children in a world designed for adults). Where the OMB/NIH categorisation *discriminates among* groups for purposes of inclusion in the provision of appropriate healthcare, racism *discriminates against* groups for purposes of othering and exclusion.

However, some campaigners point to the danger of racism feeding off what are intended to be positive distinction-drawings, and also to the danger that these latter might conceal actual racist sentiments. And it is very likely that both happen. How is one to distinguish between positive discrimination and negative discrimination to guard against this? Doing so requires considering the question of the difference between equality and fairness. To treat people equally is not always to treat them fairly. An athlete requires 5,000 calories a day, a little old lady perhaps 1,600 calories a day. To oblige both to consume the median 3,300 calories is to do an injustice to both. The point generalises across many situations. Medical research, which historically focused on men as the 'type' of human being, has come to recognise that the kind and quantity of medication suitable for men is not invariably suitable for women. To treat men and women equally in this regard is to do an injustice – is to be unfair – to women. When distinguishing between the needs of an athlete and an old lady, or between medical regimes for men and women, the key is determining what is in the best interests of the parties. If that is the aim, hidden prejudices are far less likely to be in play. If distinguishing between persons or groups where the interests of one side are purposely subjugated to that of the other or disadvantaged relative to the other, the situation is one of injustice. This latter is universally the case in racism. Both positive and negative discrimination turn on detectable differences, but the grounds and purposes of each are utterly contrasting. In the one case the difference is recognised for specific purposes, in the other for general purposes; the former is intended to good effect, in the latter the effect, intended or not, is negative – it is unjust and harmful.

These points provide material for testing whether racism is involved. Actual cases of discrimination intended to good effect have, however, been much vexed. Consider 'affirmative action' in universities, admitting candidates from historically disadvantaged groups in preference to candidates from historically advantaged groups whose test scores are higher.[5] The aim is to rectify the historical disadvantage, and to improve matters for the given group (that is: for members of the group) by providing opportunities for candidates and role models for potential candidates, lifting the horizon for all members of the group thereby. Candidates from the advantaged group who are denied a place because it has been filled by an 'affirmative action' candidate with lower admissions scores feel aggrieved; they have been unfairly treated; they demand equality of consideration for all candidates based on merit. It is characteristic of a dilemma that the arguments on both sides have much weight; and this is just such a dilemma.

Moreover, when the disadvantaged and advantaged groups differ 'by race' – by skin colour – some in the former group might feel that affirmative action is itself a form of racial condescension, and thus a form of racism in itself, while some in the latter group might feel that they are being discriminated against racially in reverse. Many in 'White' movements in the US and elsewhere feel this way, potentiated by their belief – their prejudice – that anyway white people are superior to non-white people; a double insult to them in their view.

So dominant was white supremacy in colonial times that some non-white people became complicit in its agenda. Skin-lightening creams and hair-straightening products are a mark of this. 'Black is beautiful' movements counter the complicity – powerfully supported by such frequently made observations as, for example, that Ethiopians are arguably the most beautiful people in the world. At the same time, critical responses to observations like this focus on the fact that such judgement is made according to standards applied by Europeans (thus, whites), who prefer e.g. nasal morphology similar to their own to that of Bantus or Aboriginal Australians. And this leads to expression of implicitly or explicitly racist assumptions such as are embodied in the question on social media, 'Are Ethiopians half-white?'[6] What is at work in all this is a set of assumptions and generalisations that do not survive scrutiny and, more to the point, are morally irrelevant. From every moral, legal, political and social standpoint, again acknowledging that these overlap, there are no grounds for treating any human being differently from any other, subject to the qualification that transparently justifiable accommodations (again e.g. sex-segregated toilets *pace* transgender issues, age considerations relating to children and the elderly, some medically relevant differences between sexes and populations) can be appropriate. Providing ways of ensuring that these cannot be construed as, or implicitly conceal, demeaning attitudes – racist, sexist or ageist – is essential.

The idea of a group *identity* in social terms is captured by the idea of *community*. This introduces greater definition into the picture, because it focuses attention on what the group, or subgroups within it with closer geographical or historical links than the wider collection of individuals they might be grouped with, see as sharing interests that are of particular relevance to them, and provide a basis for action. The long-term disadvantaging effects of slavery and subsequent segregation under Jim Crow laws underlie the sense of an African

RIGHT(S) AND WRONG(S)

American community in the US, and post-Civil Rights endeavours include the idea that it, as a community, is in justice owed consideration in light of them. Affirmative action in education, and the movement for reparations, are significant examples of such endeavours. The observation that groups have *interests*, chief among them the *rights* of their individual members, is intensified by a group's perception of itself as a community. This is important, because it is as a community that organisation and concerted action can better take place. Redressing historical wrongs, and in particular remedying their often serious lingering effects is important, not just for the health of the overall society in which the community is one among a number of others, but because it is the individuals constituting it who, in practical ways, suffer those effects. A signal example of community expression is 'Juneteenth', marking the liberation of slaves in the US on 19 June 1865, and made a federal holiday by Congress in 2021 in response to the Black Lives Matter movement spurred by the death of George Floyd. It had been a state holiday in Texas since 1980, with all but South Dakota following suit in the subsequent decades, but making it a federal holiday is a step forward.

***

Threading through all these points is the idea of rights, and correlatively of the wrongs that denial of them causes.

A first pass on the concepts of *human rights* and civil liberties can be made as follows. Human rights are the rights to be accorded to human individuals simply on the basis of their being human, independently of what socio-political regime they live under. They are universal. *Civil liberties* are rights that are endowed constitutionally by law upon individuals in a socio-political structure. They are particular to that structure. The concepts of human rights and civil liberties largely overlap, but are not coterminous. A right to a fair trial is a human right, but whereas in some jurisdictions (e.g. the US) an indicted person has the right to remain silent under accusation without prejudice to his case, in others (e.g. the UK) remaining silent under accusation can prejudice his case.[7] The right to unprejudicial silence is thus a civil liberty where it exists, and not a human right. In the US civil liberties are protected by the Constitution, in the UK by Common Law and statute.

The idea of universal human rights was formalised in the UN's Universal Declaration of Human Rights in 1948, and subsequently – much expanded – in its two International Covenants on Civil and Political Rights and on Economic, Social and Cultural Rights respectively. It has its long roots in the idea of 'natural rights' which in turn is derived from the idea of 'natural law', the latter going back as far as the Stoics in the third century BCE and Roman jurisprudence. 'Natural rights' were invoked in the American and French revolutions of the eighteenth century, nominated in the latter as 'the Rights of Man', but at the same time were challenged by thinkers such as David Hume and Jeremy Bentham, the latter going so far as to describe the idea of them as 'nonsense on stilts' on the grounds that rights can only be created by positive law – that is, by legislation.[8]

RIGHT(S) AND WRONG(S)

Bentham's objection to ideas of natural law and natural rights turned on the consideration that whereas legislation is a fact, the outcome of a process that can be witnessed and verified, there is no empirical ground for identifying supposed 'natural' antecedents of laws and rights. Theoreticians of them had claimed their source in a somewhat vague conception of a *logos*, by which the Stoics of antiquity meant 'a right order of things', or, which later thinkers used to mean the commandments of a deity. But one can indeed recover empirical grounds for ideas about natural law and rights, by noting the existence of moral instincts about fairness, combined with common knowledge of factors that conduce to flourishing or its opposite in human experience. Instincts about fairness are observable in non-human animals too; monkeys and dogs, for just two examples, display them.[9] Its presence across species, and natural occurrence among small children, mark it as an evolved instinct. It is easy to imagine our remotest ancestors accepting that differences in treatment, or in disbursements of resources, required a justification, perhaps allowing the chief a bigger slice of meat at the feast just because he was the chief, or to the hunters who had brought the meat home; but otherwise, in the absence of such grounds, not tolerating unfair allocations – unfair, note; not necessarily unequal – for good evolutionary reasons. In a group depending daily for survival on the effective functioning of relationships within it, such as division of labour, sharing, and other mutualities, implicit principles governing the relationships would readily emerge. No doubt, powerful individuals or subgroups would soon bend the principles to their advantage, the resulting allocations favouring them systematically. The roots of hierarchy and social inequality almost certainly lie there.[10] But greed and instincts for hoarding – appearing in more recent history as the amassing of wealth – have not expunged the instinct for fairness from the human endowment.

A direct way of justifying claims about rights is as a reaction to atrocity and suffering – the reaction of refusing to accept that the commission of atrocities and the imposition of suffering has any warrant. The refusal arises immediately from the common knowledge about what generally conduces to flourishing and its opposite in human experience. This is the justification for the UN Universal Declaration. It was a response to what happened in the 1930s and 1940s, recapitulating but at an even larger scale the harms done to people in conflicts throughout history: terror, cruelty, starvation, injury, death, grief, and the destruction of the social fabric. The assertion that subjection to such harms is intolerable and that perpetration of them should be outlawed needs no supporting argument: the facts argue for themselves. As one can match the jagged edges of two halves of a torn sheet of paper, so one can read from either the record of what happened in that period, or from the articles of the UN Declaration, what is at stake in the principles embodied in the latter.

The UN Declaration states that all individuals have a right to life, liberty and security of person, and should not be subjected to slavery, torture or cruel or degrading punishment; and that they should be recognised as persons equal before the law and entitled to its protection, secure from arbitrary arrest and imprisonment and, presumed innocent until

RIGHT(S) AND WRONG(S)

found otherwise, entitled to mount a defence. It states that they should not be subjected to arbitrary interference in their private lives, should be able to move freely within the borders of their country and free to leave and return to it – and if necessary to seek asylum elsewhere from persecution in it. It states that all individuals have the following entitlements: to freedom of thought, conscience, opinion and expression, and correlatively to gather and impart information; to assemble peacefully with others, while at the same time being free from compulsion to join any association; to participate in government either directly or through representatives freely chosen in periodic and genuine elections; to seek employment for a fair wage; to have opportunities for leisure; and to receive the support of the community if, through incapacity, they are unable to secure the means of life for themselves.

An examination of these provisions shows what they are intended to do, namely, open and preserve a space within which individuals can have a decent existence. They are of course subject to the qualification that relevant rights might be suspended in the case of individuals who violate the rights of others, and one article – the Twenty-Ninth – observes that each individual has duties to the community, in particular the duty to respect others' rights.

Most of the Declaration's articles rely on a general understanding of its key expressions, which means that more precise determination of their meaning and implications is left open. For example, a 'right to life' cannot merely mean a right to bare existence, such that if one is locked in a small cage and fed bread and water only (though this would be proscribed under the 'cruel and inhumane treatment' provision), one's right to life is being respected. A 'right to life' implies 'a minimum quality of life', and other articles flesh out this implication. In 'right to die' legal cases in the UK, in which indemnity against prosecution has been sought by people wishing to comply with a request by someone to help her die because she is suffering unbearably from an incurable condition, the courts have persistently rejected the argument that a right to die is actually entailed in the right to life on this 'life means minimum quality of life' ground.[11] Among other things this shows that the articles of the Declaration and other human rights instruments – they all share much in common – require philosophical and jurisprudential explication.

Even so, it is clear that rights entail duties and responsibilities, principally the duty to respect others' rights, but it is important to note that not all rights are correlative with duties. Some rights-bearers are not duty-bearers: babies and people who do not have, or have lost, rational faculties have rights, but we do not hold them responsible for anything. Here a useful distinction can be drawn: between moral *agents* and moral *patients*. Agents are persons (recall that this is a forensic notion, comprising rational human individuals and corporate persons) who act accountably, and patients are any entities who or which can be impacted, whether positively or negatively, by the actions of moral agents; they are entities deserving of moral regard. Moral agents are also moral patients, but the class of moral patients is far larger than the class of moral agents. For example, chickens are moral patients in virtue of being able to experience pain and fear, and something counts as a good form of existence for chickens, but of course, having no duties to other moral patients, or responsibilities of any kind, they are not moral agents.

A significant consequence of this distinction bears on the question of 'group rights'. There is a slide from recognising that groups have interests, chiefly in defending and advancing the rights of their members, to the idea that groups themselves have rights *qua* groups. A parallel slide has occurred with phrases such as 'national self-determination' and 'cultural rights'. They appear to premise, or just to be, the idea of group rights. For example, one thinks with great and justified sympathy of the injustice done to the Kurdish people – by the British after the First World War, and by the Turks, Iranians and Iraqis since – in being denied their own state. One thinks with great and justified sympathy of Tibetans and Uighurs under Chinese rule. In these and numerous other cases the idea of self-determination, autonomy, as a people – as a group – not only appears to be right but is right. Why? Because the group – the people, the 'nation' – can as a collective protect and enhance the rights of individuals within it, more effectively than if these individuals are, too often forcibly, aggregated with a larger (or in some cases smaller but more powerful) collective whose members have interests and desires that do not align with individuals in the given group. It is the *interest* of the group that its members' *right* to decide, together, how to live should be respected that gives content to the ideas of 'national self-determination' and 'cultural rights'. These are shorthand expressions of this point.

DISCRIMINATIONS

A point also therefore needs to be made about the terms 'people' and 'nation'. The latter term, in its modern sense, is an artefact mainly of the nineteenth century (though the post-1648 'Westphalian Settlement' laid the foundations),[12] and is associated with the largely negative concept of 'nationalism', an idea productive of bitter divisions and outright war. One of its ironies is that most states have different 'peoples' within their borders, and many 'nations' claim as members people who live in more than one state – as happened when Nazi Germany regarded Austrians and colinguals in Bohemia's Sudetenland as members of the same nation, and on that basis justified the Austrian *Anschluss* and annexation of the Sudetenland. Russia's activities in Ukraine, Moldova and Georgia have geopolitical and economic motives mainly, but in some cases claim that people in the occupied region identify as being or wishing to be part of the Russian nation.

'People' is a more definite term, denoting a sufficient degree of linguistic and cultural commonalities, although even here a problem remains; the World Court justice Ivor Jennings captured the problem in his remark, 'The people cannot decide until somebody decides who are the people.'[13] For it depends how finely the idea of linguistic and cultural commonalities is perceived. On one measure all occupants of the British Isles are a people, broadly sharing a language and a number of cultural features (a closely shared history, minutiae such as a proclivity for tea prepared in a way different from Indians and Chinese), while on other measures the Scots, Irish, Welsh, even the northern and southern English, noticeably differ in quotidian cultural features and linguistic idioms (and the same might be repeated for differences within the first three peoples themselves). In the US New Englanders, New Yorkers, Californians and Bible Belt southerners are in many respects noticeably unlike in outlook and matters of quotidian culture, even in linguistic ways, while Canadians, *pace* their own internal differences, share much with and differ much from their neighbours south of the Forty-Ninth Parallel. One could go on to even more marked examples in South America and Africa, in India, and in Han-derived parts of China, where linguistic differences are even more marked. Who are 'the people', which are 'the peoples'? Again, the term 'people' in democracy theory's 'will of the people' only means 'the enfranchised' – those with a vote (those not otherwise disqualified over a certain age). Variations in use by context multiply.

All this said, it remains that most people living in, say, Slovakia are culturally and linguistically different in palpable ways from most people living in, say, Venezuela, and obliging one of these 'peoples' to conform to the norms and practices of the other would require remarkably strong justification, or circumstances of *force majeure*. Yet individual Slovakians and Venezuelans can work together, marry, form friendships, learn each other's ways and tastes, on the basis of something that the whole people of the earth share: human commonalities.

The separation of the whole people of the earth into 'peoples' or 'nations', and certainly into 'states', doubtless has its roots in tribes and these in turn in the small bands hypothesised to be the social form of humanity's earliest ancestors. The amplified carry-over from the earliest forms of social

DISCRIMINATIONS

organisation, together with changes to those forms prompted by increased numbers and the opportunities that consequently came into view for enterprising individuals, have their current expression as a result. It cannot be said that it is a uniformly happy one, as the perpetual scar of war on human history attests.

An examination of the UN's International Covenant on Civil and Political Rights, adopted in 1966, is instructive from the viewpoint of the muddle caused by talking collectively of 'peoples'. It begins, in its Preamble, 'Considering that, in accordance with the principles proclaimed in the Charter of the United Nations, recognition of the inherent dignity and of the equal and inalienable rights of all members of the human family is the foundation of freedom, justice and peace in the world; Recognizing that these rights derive from the inherent dignity of the human person … Realizing that the individual, having duties to other individuals and to the community to which he belongs, is under a responsibility to strive for the promotion and observance of the rights recognized in the present Covenant' and then, in Article 1, immediately jumps to asserting, 'All peoples have the right of self-determination. By virtue of that right they freely determine their political status and freely pursue their economic, social and cultural development.' The jump from individual rights to the 'right of peoples' is made without definition of 'peoples' or comment on the relation between the rights inhering in individuals to their putative collective right as 'a people'. Evidently the unexpressed assumption, a justified one, is that the rights of individuals are better protected and enhanced by their combining to form organisations to achieve this end, the rights of individuals being the fundamental thing from which all else derives. An articulation of this would proceed by iterating the right of assembly and recognising the advantage of individuals working together so that each of them can enjoy all the other individual rights listed in the Universal Declaration. A formulation that made explicit the point of protecting the endeavours of individuals who work in concert to this end would need no adventitious introduction of 'peoples' nor the fallacy of composition to 'peoples' having rights.

In fact, the drafting of the 1966 Covenant has an unfortunate implication, which is that it provides an excuse to anyone claiming to act on behalf of 'the people' to suppress the rights of individuals in the interests of 'the rights of the people' (think of the Politburo of the former Soviet Union, or today's North Korea, for prime examples). Note the date of the Covenant, 1966; it was adopted in the midst of decolonisation around the world, and served to strengthen independence movements from colonial powers – in itself a good thing – but too many of the newly independent states adhered to borders drawn by their former colonial masters, borders which corralled together people who, in other circumstances, might have preferred to serve – through collective action – their individual rights in their own way differently from others they were corralled with. Tensions between Sinhalese and Tamils in Sri Lanka, formerly Ceylon, are just one example of what too often therefore occurred. The Covenant was drafted *de haut en bas*, in geopolitical terms, and not in terms of the texture of local realities and what these meant for the rights of the very individuals from whom its Preamble draws the conception of rights itself.

The point of labouring this is that the discourse of 'group rights' has come to distort what is or should be the focal concern in achieving greater justice in the world. This is that no individual should be subjected to negative discrimination and the exclusions it causes. Prejudice of all kinds – racist, sexist, ageist, and against LGBTQ+ people – is by its nature a 'grouping' phenomenon, but each and every one of its victims is an individual whose rights are compromised by it. To understand the effects of prejudice is primarily to understand the effects on individuals and only *via* them to the communities they form. Waking to the effects of prejudice might be prompted by seeing its cumulative impact on communities – for example, in the case of African Americans in the US in localities troubled by poverty, crime, substance abuse and deficits of education and health (such at any rate is the stereotype, far from universally true but true enough to be a concern – as, note, are localities with the same socio-economic profile populated mainly by white residents). Reversing or at least mitigating such effects requires lifting individuals out of poverty and lowering barriers that exclude them from opportunities and participations. These can only happen to and for individuals, even if the provision of clinics, schools and job opportunities is framed as a remedy for 'the community' – which indeed it is, in the shorthand way we have of speaking about these matters; but the remedy works, and can only work, via the benefit to individuals.

As long as reference to groups is understood as a shorthand for talk about the individual people who constitute them, no harm is done. But when 'the group' is the entity, a variety of complications arise. For example, in the decades preceding this writing, atrocities by religiously motivated individuals (for a salient example, the 9/11 attack on the World Trade Center in New York and the Pentagon in Washington) galvanised renewed criticism by secularists and atheists of religious beliefs and organisations, notable among the proponents of this movement Richard Dawkins and Christopher Hitchens.[14] In the acerbic debates that surrounded the publication of their and others' views, distinctions became important, principally between individuals with a faith commitment and religious beliefs, organisations and movements. A Christian – an individual human being – is one thing, his beliefs, his Church, are another; individual Christians are not all alike, and neither are Christian sects and denominations. Likewise it is important to distinguish between the Islamic religion and its various sects, and 'Islamism', a catch-all term for activist political and military endeavours to defend the faith, or to punish impugners, or to assert dominance. In this case the distinction between individuals, on the one hand, and on the other hand beliefs and organisations or movements, matters.

Believers seek to defend against attacks on their beliefs – which is to say, on the religion itself – by construing them as a hate crime; and in some places (for example, the UK) this has been achieved. Because the beliefs and the religion are the same thing, the former constituting the latter, we see how tendentiously this version of an appeal to 'group rights' works. Whereas the right of any individual, whether a religious believer or not, to freedom of thought, conscience, opinion and expression is asserted in all human rights instruments, and whereas *qua* individual a religious person has the same right as anyone else to be treated with respect until he forfeits it by violating the rights of others, only the same kind of extrapolation from individuals to 'peoples' at work in the UN's 1966 Covenant permits the slide from the believer to the religion. Would we accept doing the same with, say, political beliefs? Because an individual has a right to hold them, do the beliefs themselves – constituting the political agenda of a party, and by transitivity the party itself – likewise 'have the right' not to be challenged, attacked, even mocked? That would be unacceptable. And in fact, the right to an opinion entails the correlative right to disagree and challenge from the viewpoint of a contrary opinion. If that is not only a right but a necessity in the political case, what justifies outlawing it in the case of religious beliefs?

Notice that legitimate candidates for protection under the rubric of 'hate crimes' are matters over which individuals have no or very little choice: their skin colour, sex, sexuality, age and disability. But an individual's religion is a matter of choice (*pace* the social compulsions which make or keep an individual a votary of it – which, note, can also apply to political sentiments). Religious beliefs are not a legitimate candidate for protection against 'hate' in the same way as sexuality or age. To repeat, *individuals* are protected by regimes of rights against discrimination on the grounds of their beliefs, yes;

and that is as it should be. But that is a different matter; their *beliefs* should not be immune to challenge, nor therefore the institutions that promote and proselytise those beliefs, any more than any other of their beliefs and opinions.

Another example, an important one, is the question of reparations for slavery. In this connection the focus has been on descendants of victims of the Atlantic slave trade between the sixteenth and nineteenth centuries, the great majority of these victims transported to the Americas, and numbering up to twelve million people. Not just the conditions of slavery themselves but the racist attitudes involved and which persisted after emancipation – one concrete expression of which were the segregationist Jim Crow laws in southern US states, not repealed until 1965, a century later; but repealing laws does not repeal attitudes – have left deep scars on descendants, burdening them with a multiplicity of economic and social disadvantages. The slave ancestry of African Americans leaves an invisible yoke round the necks and chains on the feet of too many of them. This is the ground for the claim to reparations – to address and remedy disabilities inherited from the slave past. It is a justified claim. The central concern is to understand what form reparations should take, whom they are to be made to, and by whom they are to be made.

On the face of it the 'whom to and whom by' questions seem straightforward. Black Americans are one clear focus; the economies – and particularly identifiable locations within them such as the slave-trade port cities of Bristol and Liverpool in England – that profited from slavery are the other. This is right, but not yet enough; many more individuals in other countries, and many more economies than those of the US and the UK, need to be included. Moreover the story of slavery, though starkly clear-cut in the North American case, is much larger and longer than this, and has to be understood for context.

It is not irrelevant that almost everyone on the planet is the descendant of both slaves and slave-owners, given the ubiquity of slavery throughout history, but this point can be set aside given that it is the malign effects of recent and painfully visible slavery that are at issue. More relevant is the fact of the Arab slave trade, considering it only since the eighth century CE under Islam though thousands of years older (it is mentioned as a commonplace in the Code of Hammurabi), and which ended only in the twentieth century – in at least its most obvious historical form; as we shall see below, slavery continues in other forms in many places and not just, to take one of several notable current examples, the United Arab Emirates. In this trade since the eighth century, counting the trans-Saharan, Indian Ocean and Red Sea routes, estimates suggest that up to twenty million individuals were enslaved.[15] A point of particular importance is that in both the Arab and Atlantic slave trades, it was Africans who captured and sold other Africans to Arabs and Europeans. The Arabs' chief suppliers were the Imbangala, Nyamwezi and Swahili; Zanzibar was for centuries the chief slave entrepôt of the east African coast. In the west of Africa the Ashanti, Yoruba and others sold slaves to ships on the Atlantic and to camel trains which crossed the Sahara to the Arab world.[16] The cruelty of the slavers was unsurpassed even by the horrendous slaving ships that made the passage to the New World.[17]

RIGHT(S) AND WRONG(S)

These considerations add complexity to the matter of who owes reparations. But it does not lessen the claim of those whose current situation is a clear consequence of fully documented slavery in recent centuries.[18] In this regard the question concerns what form reparations should take. For example, some claim that cash should be paid to today's US descendants of slaves; estimates as to the quantum vary from $200,000 to $1 million for each African American US citizen.[19] A major impetus for thinking along these lines is that reparations were in fact paid in cash (or interest-yielding long-term government securities) to slave-*owners* when emancipation occurred; a number of wealthy families today owe that wealth to what their forebears were paid by way of compensation.[20] 'Compensation': the bitterness of the irony is almost too much to bear.

But the idea of cash reparations paid to individual descendants of slaves faces objections, obvious and otherwise, and does not really address what is caused by the damaging legacy of slavery. The more valid point was well made by a Bristol councillor, Cleo Lake, at the time of debate in that city – a slave-trade port – associated with the commemoration of the UK's 1807 abolition of the slave trade: 'Reparations is not a paycheque for the descendants of people who were enslaved, it is a process outlined by the UN which looks for holistic repair. This can include public apologies, social justice initiatives, education or cultural projects, commemorative ceremonies, affirmative action and much more.'[21] The same is more fully encapsulated in the ten-point reparations plan put forward by the Caribbean Community (CARICOM) in respect of effects on descendants of slaves there, but adds a workable suggestion on the financial front: international debt cancellation and investment in the form of technology transfer.[22]

Even more to the point, a powerful way to make up for the history of slavery is to combat today's slavery. The International Labour Organization (ILO) estimates that fifty million people live in slavery today, twenty-eight million of them in various forms of forced labour (defined as 'all work or service which is exacted from any person under the menace of any penalty and for which the said person has not offered himself voluntarily') and twenty-two million in forced marriage.[23] Counting all the different forms that slavery takes, this is undoubtedly a conservative estimate. Sex trafficking, bonded labour, debt bondage, child labour, child soldiers, incarceration in labour camps (often without trial under terms of 'Administrative Detention' in China), domestic service under inhumane conditions relating to any or all of hours, wages, tasks and accommodation, indeed any work under such conditions (as experienced by labourers shipped into the United Arab Emirates typically from south Asia), are all forms of slavery. These categories fall within the ILO definition of 'forced labour', but the vulnerable circumstances of many people expose them to exploitation in ways that too closely approximate the same, effectively making them slaves to economic conditions, for example those in which employment practices occur that take advantage of the combination of plentiful labour supply and high poverty levels.[24]

***

RIGHT(S) AND WRONG(S)

The bearing of these discussions on the 'group rights' issue is the same in both cases. In the religion case, it is individuals who have a right not to be discriminated against on grounds of their religion, because they have a right to hold their beliefs; it is not their beliefs – which is to say by transitivity, the religion constituted by them – that have a 'right to be immune from challenge and criticism'. By the same token it is each individual descendant of recent slavery victims in the US and Caribbean who are the intended beneficiaries of the reparation endeavours described. Summative accounts, for example in statistical generalisations over communities, neighbourhoods, people in education or employment, and the like, talk of groups or populations, but by their nature are insufficiently fine-grained to register that some of the individuals summed over are successful, wealthy and well. Group-talk is a version of the rhetorical device of *synecdoche*, where the whole does duty for the parts – the parts in this case being individuals. The synecdochal referent – the thing referred to by the group term – is then *hypostasised* – treated as a 'real' thing. But the real things are individuals. Accordingly when one talks of the interests of a group, for example in saying 'reparations are in the interest of African Americans' or 'Brexit damaged the interests of the British people', the truth of what is said is a function of the benefit or detriment accrued to the individuals thus collectively referred to.

This point matters crucially in the final two chapters below. There, it will be clear that arguing that rights appertain exclusively to individuals does not entail 'individualism' in the socio-political sense advocated by, for a chief example, libertarians.

***

What of the problem of conflicts of rights? What of the fact that the interests of society require a balancing of competing interests of individuals? As agents, individuals have a duty to respect the rights of others; as sharers of a social domain which benefits from mutualities and co-operation, they have an interest in avoiding such conflicts, or having means of resolving them when they occur. There are circumstances when society has an interest in depriving some or even all its members of their rights – for example in punishing criminals, or limiting freedom of expression in time of war – but such actions require unimpeachable justification. Individuals might recognise the necessity of bearing with suspension of some of their rights in specific cases, though it is a different matter when a society denies rights absolutely, which is a defining feature of oppressive regimes. In a liberal dispensation any suspension of rights requires not only an overwhelming justification but also limits in extent and – except for very specific circumstances, such as life sentences for extremely grave crimes – time; if interference with rights is necessitated by, say, a major emergency such as war or pandemic, the justification for it has to come with a 'sunset clause'.

The distinction between rights and interests is important here. Individuals and groups have interests which can and often do conflict with the interests of others, and given that both the interests and the conflicts are of many different kinds, many different ways of adjudicating them exist. For example, conflicts of interest among commercial companies competing in the same market will in the end be resolved by which of them is more successful in attracting customers, but if one tries to subvert the activities of competitors by other means there is, if relevant, the recourse of law.

Is 'not being offended' an interest or a right? Obviously it is the former; equally obviously, it is not the latter. We have an interest in not being offended or insulted because it is unpleasant to be so, and when especially barbed, it can do us hurt. Gratuitous offence-giving is rude, ill-mannered, anti-social; the normal response to ill-manners is to eschew the boor and limit courtesies by return. But the debate is not about ill manners, it is about holding views and engaging in practices that cause feelings of offence and hurt in those who disagree. But that one person's disagreement with and challenge to another's views and practices offends the latter does not give the latter the right to silence the former. It is frequently pointed out that 'feeling offended' is a subjective matter, whereas a wound on the body is objective. It is pointed out in return, correctly, that psychological hurts can be no different – or even worse – than bodily hurts, and longer-lasting. The response to this, in turn, and also correctly, is that psychological hurts are inevitabilities of the human condition – think of disappointment, grief, anxiety and depression – and being disagreed with, objected to and rejected by others are inevitabilities of the social condition. Though we have interests in avoiding psychological hurts, we do not have 'a right' to avoid them, any more than we have a right to be physically in two different places at the same time. People who disagree might each feel offended by the other's views; which of them has the right to silence the other? We would not think that (say) the older, or better-educated, or taller, or better-looking, has such a right; why would a person – other than one with a specific kind of involuntary identity; see below – thereby have the right to deny others their right to the possession and expression of their views?

The concept of 'hate crime' appears to endow a right not to be offended. The appearance is the result of the shorthand effect of gathering the justifications for outlawing hate speech under a rubric. All but one of the categories of persons protected by hate speech laws (the outlier is religion, which has no place here because religious commitment is *au fond* a voluntary matter) relate to involuntary conditions – acknowledging that certain kinds of medical interventions can make them different – viz. sex, sexuality, age, 'race' (in effect, skin colour and constitutive aspects of ethnicity) and disability. The purpose of the laws is to protect against discrimination, which means ensuring observation of the right of individual persons in these categories to equal consideration as full members of the human community, which is specifically what talk of 'respect' and 'inherent dignity of the human person' means in human rights discourse. On the principle of taking a mile from an inch, the logic of the offence agenda extends 'hate speech' to disagreement with or challenge to any views, sentiments, choices, self-identifications or affiliations dear to the possessor of them. The logic of this reveals the problem. At the limit it would entail that the term 'respect' in human rights discourse confers a general right to silence others if they disagree with or challenge one's views and choices. Were this so, I should 'respect' and therefore not voice disagreement with, or challenge, anyone whose views I regard as harmful.

This comes down to accepting that one cannot regard the objective of winning an argument, or succeeding in a campaign, as justification for denying the rights of others to the expression of their views. Given that some views are horrible, or appear horrible from one's own standpoint, this seems a big ask; the temptation to prevent their expression in order to stop them becoming influential is a very natural one. But there is a point of principle, and a point of practicality, to be made about this. The point of principle is that the way to deal with horrible views is to challenge them, refute them with better argument and evidence, expose fallacies in them, show what ill-consequences of their application are or would be, demonstrate that they merit rejection and even ridicule. The point of practicality is that silencing views drives them underground where they can and usually do fester and become more toxic and thus more dangerous. One does better to know what someone's views are than to silence him. The combination of these points together with the fact that, in combatting horrible views, one is relying on one's own right to have views and express them, is conclusive. With the exception of hate speech, imposing silence is neither the right nor the *rights* way to go.

This point also matters crucially in the final two chapters below.

***

The point about psychological hurt is frequently associated with talk of fragility and vulnerability. Individuals in oppressed circumstances have a claim in this regard, though critics of the 'woke agenda' are quick to run *ad hominem* arguments against – for a chief example of their targets – the young from privileged circumstances who become activists in the agenda's various causes, and adopt some of the fragility defences at issue. That the arguments are *ad hominem* makes them irrelevant to determining whether the causes have merit; rather, the fact that young people from privileged circumstances adopt them is itself a matter of merit.

Two rather different points are at issue here. The obvious one is that many if not most proponents of the agenda themselves come from the oppressed circumstances at issue. The Black Lives Matter campaign, the Me Too campaign, the campaign for transgender recognition, were started and are conducted by people whose motives derive from personal experience of what prompted them. That they draw allies from people not in the same boat does credit to those allies. It is heartening to see this. In general terms it is also heartening to see that the tradition continues of young people kicking against the traces of their societies; flexing consciences, engaging rather than merely observing, trying to make a difference. There is a conventional story about how, after marching in demonstrations and yelling slogans, the young inevitably grow older and cease to do these things as the sobering pressure of jobs, families and mortgages exerts itself. Successive generations have gone through this cycle. Some of the 'anti-woke warriors' – at times almost hysterical in their claim that the 'woke agenda' threatens the demise of civilisation (specifically, Western civilisation; see the next chapter) – appear to be blind to this aspect of the matter.

But – the second point – there is claimed to be a difference in the young of the woke-wars era. Generalisations impend, though perhaps not without substance. They amount to saying that today's young – 'Gen Z' in the relevant term of art – are less robust, more fragile, more vulnerable, in need of trigger warnings, safe spaces, coddling, protection from unpleasant realities.[25] To some critics they seem to wish to share an experience of suffering with those they care about and campaign alongside. To other, less mordant, critics they seem to be at risk of being unprepared for the rough realities that characterise life in a multivarious world. The problem in education is taken to be acute; if exposure to challenging and difficult ideas is limited or muffled, a consequence will be to disarm them in the face of the rough realities in question. The lack of sympathy 'anti-wokists' have for the causes that give rise to 'wokism' too often extends *ad hominem* to those experiencing them, as well as their allies and supporters. When this happens, generalisations are doing too much work.

6

CONCERNS AND COMPARISONS

A comparison between the 'PC wars' of the 1990s and the 'woke wars' of the 2020s, a generation apart, shows how little has changed, how much has changed, what has not changed enough, and what is new, in respect of racism, sexism, sexualities and gender identity. A full survey would include ageism and ableism too. The following remarks apply to the Anglo-Saxon world; it is likely that in everything other than racism, the advances have been greater in western and northern Europe.

What is new is the scope and nature of discussions about sexualities and gender. As regards the first, the traditional hetero–homo binary, which admitted bisexuality as a marginal third path, has broadened across a range of sexual expressions and choices; sexual fluidity and diversity of orientation have become recognised and more accepted.[1]

As regards the second, matters have not advanced quite so much. For those whose early-assigned gender does not match what they are, possibilities for living their real gender have widened, with an increased range of medical gender-affirmation options in aid for those who choose them.[2] A leading reason is sensitivity over women's spaces, imposing more of a brake on acceptance than in the case of sexual fluidity. Although a generation ago – certainly until the 1990s – medical gender-affirmation methods had become advanced, and debates about gender from Simone de Beauvoir through Judith Butler onwards had furthered understanding of the degree to which it is a socially constructed concept, general attitudes to it continued to be less than sympathetic, and the number of individuals fully taking the opportunity to live their gender remained limited. Attitudes and opportunities have improved since then, but as the women's-spaces issue shows, they are still subject to controversy.[3]

Feminism has achieved advances in the world's most developed societies, which have the highest female participation in public and economic life. This is historically the result of development rather than its cause; but arguably development would not have been sustainable without it, given that having the skill potential of half the population unavailable or at least limited would constitute a brake on it. But even in these places women's earnings still lag noticeably behind those of men, by an average of 16%. In the US more women than men gain university degrees (57% to 43%) but are still in a minority in the upper reaches of science, education and public life. They not only earn less when they get there, but have a significantly harder time doing so.[4]

The global picture is yet worse: according to UN figures, 66% of the world's work is done by women, who produce

DISCRIMINATIONS

50% of its food yet earn only 10% of its income and own only 1% of its property. However much better things are for women in advanced economies, the shape of the pattern is similar.

There are many reasons for this situation. A main one is structural – and structures embody and reflect attitudes. In advanced economies the 9 a.m. to 5 p.m. pattern of the paid working day is largely inimical to family life, making it difficult for women who have domestic commitments to combine them with access to what the male-oriented world regards as economically rewardable. At the same time women's vital contributions in child-rearing, home-making and providing unpaid care are grossly undervalued. In some communities in advanced countries, religious attitudes sequester women to the domestic sphere entirely. In these cases the barriers faced are exacerbated by the general fact that women are subjected far more than men to abuse and violence.

The existence of equality laws has, therefore, still not achieved their aim, as the points about the US above show. The injustice experienced by women in these respects creates and perpetuates a multiplicity of problems by the skewing of political and economic activity in the direction of what might well be called masculine tendencies and outcomes: profit above human or environmental concerns, competition, aggression and war. To put the matter graphically: it is a remarkable propaganda success, in historical terms, that women have been encouraged to bear and raise children so that those children can end up as battlefield corpses; if women were full participants in deciding such matters, it is likely that there would be fewer such corpses and all that they symbolise.[5]

CONCERNS AND COMPARISONS

Traditional arguments in justification of the disparities between men and women in public and economic terms turn principally on considerations of reproductive biology. The differences appealed to are a datum, but a better-organised society would value them appropriately and accommodate itself to their exigencies. The working day, the working week, could be made flexible enough to reflect this; as it is, women have to earn less or fall behind in their careers because the corporate week is still too rigid, despite adjustments latterly made. While accommodating women's life patterns is regarded as a favour – in effect, a condescension – by the male-oriented order, the structure of work continues to embody discrimination, preserving the superior access enjoyed by men to resources of the kind most valued in male-oriented society.

As regards racism an immediate distinction has to be drawn between *racism* and the *effects* of racism. Taking the US experience as a salient example, one has to ask what to infer about racism as such from the fact that there has been progress, in a number of respects, in relation to its effects.

Metrics for the participation of African Americans in economic and public life in the US show a significant advance over the situation a generation ago, which indicates that the force of systemic factors has lessened to some degree.[6] A generation ago, in the 1990s, a Brookings Institution report could state this:

> In 1940, 60% of employed black women worked as domestic servants; today [1998] the number is down to 2.2%, while 60%

hold white-collar jobs. In 1958, 44% of whites said they would move if a black family became their next door neighbor; today the figure is 1%. In 1964, the year the great Civil Rights Act was passed, only 18% of whites claimed to have a friend who was black; today 86% say they do, while 87% of blacks assert they have white friends ... More than 40% of African Americans now consider themselves members of the middle class. 42% own their own homes, a figure that rises to 75% if we look just at black married couples. Black two-parent families earn only 13% less than those who are white. Almost a third of the black population lives in suburbia. Because these are facts the media seldom report, the black underclass continues to define black America in the view of much of the public. Many assume blacks live in ghettos, often in high-rise public housing projects. Crime and the welfare check are seen as their main source of income. The stereotype crosses racial lines. Blacks are even more prone than whites to exaggerate the extent to which African Americans are trapped in inner-city poverty. In a 1991 Gallup poll, about one-fifth of whites, but almost half of black respondents, said that at least three out of four African Americans were impoverished urban residents. And yet, in reality, blacks who consider themselves middle class outnumber those with incomes below the poverty line by a wide margin.[7]

This 1998 survey of progress relating to the *effects* of racism looks rosy. A 2018 report by the Economic Policy Institute (EPI), itself surveying the previous fifty years, considerably tempers that glow.[8] The EPI study looked back over the period since the publication of the 1968 Kerner Commission report on civil disorder in African American communities, and its headline states, 'African Americans are better off in many ways but are still disadvantaged by racial inequality'. For whereas African Americans had advanced in absolute terms in most of the respects identified by the Brookings figures, in others they had actually lost ground.

The EPI reports its key findings thus:

African Americans today are much better educated than they were in 1968 but still lag behind whites in overall educational attainment. More than 90 percent of younger African Americans (ages 25 to 29) have graduated from high school, compared with just over half in 1968 – which means they've nearly closed the gap with white high school graduation rates. They are also more than twice as likely to have a college degree as in 1968 but are still half as likely as young whites to have a college degree.

The substantial progress in educational attainment of African Americans has been accompanied by significant absolute improvements in wages, incomes, wealth, and health since 1968. But black workers still make only 82.5 cents on every dollar earned by white workers, African Americans are 2.5 times as likely to be in poverty as whites, and the median white family has almost ten times as much wealth as the median black family.

With respect to homeownership, unemployment, and incarceration, America has failed to deliver any progress for African Americans over the last five decades. In these areas, their situation has either failed to improve relative to whites or has worsened. In 2017 the black unemployment rate was 7.5 percent, up from 6.7 percent in 1968, and is still roughly twice the white unemployment rate. In 2015, the black homeownership rate was just over 40 percent, virtually unchanged since 1968, and trailing a full thirty points behind the white homeownership rate, which saw modest gains over the same period. And the share of African Americans in prison or jail almost tripled between 1968 and 2016 and is currently more than six times the white incarceration rate.[9]

The actual numbers give these generalisations bite. In 2018 the wealth of a 'typical black family' was $17,500 – six times higher than 1968's $2,500 figure – but looks very different from the wealth of a median white family at $171,000. Home ownership, which Brookings had picked out as a significant marker of progress, had scarcely changed in reality: 41.1% in 1968, 41.2% in 2018. This compares to 71.1% for whites. Over the surveyed period health improved dramatically for African Americans, with infant mortality dropping from 34.9 deaths per 1,000 in 1968 to 11.4 by 2018 (the respective white rates are 18.8 and 4.9), but whereas in 1968 black infants were 1.9 times more likely to die than white infants, in 2018 they were 2.3 times more likely. African American life expectancy increased by 11.5 years between 1968 and 2018, but by the latter date was still 3.5 years less than for a white person.[10]

In a comment published in January 2020, Sharon Wright Austin, a professor of political science at the University of Florida, noted what side of the debate about institutional racism (*vide* Ta-Nehisi Coates, Michelle Alexander) versus

'African Americans have to take personal responsibility' (*vide* Ben Carson, Thomas Sowell) would be taken by Martin Luther King Jr – namely, the former.[11] Dr King had practical suggestions for addressing the problem, detailed in the moral vision of his 'Economic Bill of Rights' proposal. In quoting King's 'Lord, we ain't what we oughta be. We ain't what we want to be. We ain't what we gonna be. But, thank God, we ain't what we was', Professor Wright Austin concludes, 'Progress has been made. Just not as much as many of us would like.'[12]

When it comes to the ugly fact of *racism* as such, this is an understatement. One can register, to leave on the desktop as it were, the fact that advances in the condition of racial minorities almost certainly serve to increase racist hostility among those who already dislike seeing encroachments into what they regard as their sphere. A factor of greater importance is that the advances themselves have empowered minorities to claim their rights and speak out more emphatically against infringements of them. Add to this the advent of the smartphone, enabling the instantaneous recording and dissemination of footage of e.g. brutality against people of colour. Moreover, racism has layers; as its effects are progressively peeled back, underlying attitudes and sentiments become exposed, so that biases, even unconscious ones, lodged with varying degrees of conscious or unconscious subtlety in language and practices, come into view; this is where, for a significant example, unintended microaggressions recognised by their targets become an issue. 'The cumulative effect', wrote Nesrine Malik in 2020, reflecting on the

Black Lives Matter movement, 'is an increased access to, and visibility in, sectors that project the message of racial inequality, particularly the media and the political sphere. Along with that comes the benefits of creating activism networks, raising funding, and signal boosting race-related causes that in the past would have depended on the efforts of a single charismatic leader, such as Martin Luther King'.[13]

Along with progress in relation to the effects of racism, therefore, has come progress in the means available for promoting the anti-racist cause. But neither has ended racism itself: very far from it. That is why Critical Race Theory (CRT) has emerged as a battleground issue, because it focuses on the structural and historical reasons for the persistence of racism as a fact, and draws the ire of conservative critics who see it as an attack on white students by making them feel bad about being white, as unpatriotic, as lying about the founding conditions of the nation, and as having poisoned roots (in Marxism and postmodernism) and poisoned fruits (threatening the values of the American way, viz. 'private property, individual rights, equality under the law, federalism, and freedom of speech').[14]

The key issues at stake in the CRT battle, and those at stake in the 'woke wars' in general – the latter covers more ground than the former, although questions of sexualities and gender arise in connection with 'intersectionality' in CRT debates – are the same for both sides of the argument. Arguments deployed by CRT critics such as conservative activist Christopher Rufo are very similar to those used by 'anti-woke' critics in general, invoking the same tropes of Marxist/

postmodernist infiltration of ideas – or worse: an explicit conspiracy to overthrow the US by their means, following a communist playbook of ways to undermine Western societies, as argued by journalist David Volodzko.[15]

These arguments require comment, offered below; first, the task of comparing the 'PC' debate of the 1990s with contemporary 'woke wars' debates merits completion.

Any sufficient social and political history of the decades after the end of the Second World War would have to embrace a global perspective. By the 1960s and 1970s Cold War tensions, the Cultural Revolution in China, anti-apartheid struggles in South Africa, the Vietnam War, campus uprisings, turmoils in France culminating in *les evénèments* of 1968, and much besides, were the broad context within which civil rights campaigns and feminism reached an intensity in the US and elsewhere that seemed to contemporaries to portend a general overthrow of the existing order. Given that the tangled roots of these occurrences were doubtless first exposed by the dislocating effect of the Second World War, and that the effort of most countries to 'restore normality' in as many respects as possible – *pace* such international developments as the United Nations and decolonisation movements, and significant national changes such as, for one example, the UK's introduction of a moderate form of socialism (the National Health Service, public ownership of coal, iron and steel production, civil aviation, railways, utilities and the Bank of England) – was at first attended with a rapid phase of prosperity, especially in the US which had gained enormously from war production and had emerged as the richest and most powerful state in the world. The paradox of progress – in this case increased prosperity, widening education, and their joint outcome of increased determination to root out structures and conditions that had led to world war and which the war had more clearly exposed – had much to do with the explosions of the 1960s.

In any event, these explosions happened; and at the same time ideas that both led to them and were prompted by them became influential in some quarters, not least those that are collected under the 'postmodernism' rubric, a number of whose leading proponents were Marxists.

Given the hostility of the US to the USSR and Communist China, and the associated 'red scare' sentiments especially on the conservative side of US politics, a mindset of suspicion of such ideas was already well established. The 'House Un-American Activities Committee', associated with the name of Joseph McCarthy but established (in 1938) before his time, had lost its influence by the 1960s, heavily criticised for its methods and its violations of First Amendment rights of those it targeted; but the anxieties and antipathies it embodied remained. It is therefore unsurprising that conservative critics of campaigns in support of civil rights, LGBTQ+ rights, abortion, equality for women, and against the Vietnam War, should collect them under the heading of a 'radical Left' threat, for the mindset was a convenient, ready-to-hand explanation of what they feared. In any case it is true that, in higher education particularly, a number of those theorising about these various struggles made use of postmodernist and sometimes more directly Marxist tropes. But it is rather doubtful that civil rights and feminist activists were reading the literature of these theoretical positions and then taking to the streets under their immediate influence. Indeed, civil rights activists had no need of them; they had their own and their history's experience to motivate them without a theory telling them what their experience was. Nevertheless, reflection on the conditions that produce discrimination finds much that is richly suggestive in analyses of power and class. When in need of an explanatory framework, headline summaries of the theories were as convenient for activists as the McCarthyite mindset was for their critics, though it is likely that these were all that most of the latter knew. And because more thorough investigation of the theories took place in universities, it was inevitable that critics of social justice movements would focus on them and claim that they were riddled with Leftists poisoning the minds of students.

A survey of academics in the period between 1969 and 1985, undertaken to see whether the turmoils of the 1960s had radicalised the academy, produced a surprising result.[16] In self-identification of political position 5.8% of faculty said they were Leftists; 33.8% said they were Liberals. The latter number represented a 6.8% decrease over the figure for 1969. Self-identified moderate and strong Conservatives constituted 29.6% and 4.2% of faculty bodies respectively, these proportions showing an increase over 1969. Perhaps most significant was the change in Left and Liberal attitudes to making university admission easier; in 1969 the move was opposed by 39.4% of this group, while by 1985 it had risen to 71.7%.[17]

DISCRIMINATIONS

Conservative critics of 'PC' focused attention on university departments where the proportions of Left and Liberal faculty were high: philosophy, sociology, history and literature. They ignored e.g. business studies (where less than 1% self-identified as Left and less than 16% identified as Liberal) and the natural sciences, whose faculty, anecdotally, are too busy and absorbed in matters removed from socio-political currents.[18] If anything, the university departments from which Wall Street and Washington – the financial and political power centres – recruited staff were praised for being what a Heritage Foundation publication described as 'immune [to] the creeping rot of multiculturalism, feminism, deconstructionism and other fashionably radical trends'.[19]

Later commentators identified the trigger for the 'anti-PC' movement as an article by Richard Bernstein in the *New York Times* in 1990: 'Most Americans had never heard of the phrase "politically correct" before 1990, when a wave of stories began to appear in newspapers and magazines. One of the first and most influential was published in October 1990 by the New York Times reporter Richard Bernstein, who warned – under the headline "The Rising Hegemony of the Politically Correct" – that the country's universities were threatened by "a growing intolerance, a closing of debate, a pressure to conform".'[20] A flood of commentary in similar vein followed, in the *Wall Street Journal* (lamenting a 'brave new world of ideological zealotry'), *Newsweek* (its cover headline 'THOUGHT POLICE'), *Time* magazine (decrying 'a new intolerance') and *New York* magazine ('The New Fascists are taking over the universities'). Television news and talk shows featured the claims prominently – on *Nightline, This Week with David Brinkley, Good Morning America, Crossfire, MacNeil/Lehrer NewsHour, Firing Line* – a debate on this last concluding that 'Freedom of Thought is in Danger on American Campuses'.

Bernstein's report was based on a visit to the Berkeley campus in California where he found an 'unofficial ideology' according to which 'a cluster of opinions about race, ecology, feminism, culture and foreign policy defines a kind of "correct" attitude to problems of the world'.[21] Although it was this article that lit the touch-paper, Bernstein had been troubled for a while; in 1989 he wrote an article comparing a Duke University conference on liberal education to the 'minute of hatred' in Orwell's *1984* (it is in the novel *two* minutes), describing professors as 'uncivil libertarians' who have a hit-list of 'enemies'.[22]

The digital database ProQuest records that the term 'politically correct' was rarely used before 1990, in that year appearing less than 800 times, but in 1991 it occurred 2,500 times and in the following year 2,800 times. The articles recycled the same stories from a few top universities. A Harvard professor, Stephan Thernstrom, was said to have been attacked and vilified by students for racially insensitive remarks, and that as he walked past Harvard Yard's 'fluttering elms he found it hard not to imagine the pointing fingers, the whispers. Racist, there goes *the racist*. It was hellish, this persecution'. In an interview shortly afterwards Thernstrom said the harassment had never happened. The source of the story was one editorial in a student newspaper which had criticised him for reading from diaries of plantation owners in his lectures. But 'the image of college students conducting witch hunts stuck'.[23]

What had begun as an ironic use of the term 'political correctness' among Leftists as a check on their own dogmatism was appropriated by conservatives, who said that it was the mark of a 'political programme that was seizing control of American universities and cultural institutions – and they were determined to stop it.'[24] The term's origins vanished into mythology; Dinesh D'Souza, giving the anti-PC campaign the authority of hardcover book publication in 1992, wrote that it 'originated in the early part of this century, when it was employed by various species of Marxists to describe and enforce conformity to preferred ideological positions', and did so without 'any sense of irony or self-deprecation'.[25]

Inevitably, conservatives claiming that PC warriors were trying to silence them sought in turn to silence the PC warriors. 'By expanding the meaning of [the term] to include *any* expression of radical ideas, conservatives ... turned it into a mechanism for doing exactly what they charged is being done to them – silencing dissenters' – one example of the process in practice was Fox Television's news director in Washington writing to the company's chairman demanding that he fire 'politically correct' employees.[26]

In short, those voicing opposition to racism, sexism, war, ecological damage and homophobia were positioned as endangering freedom of speech and thought, threatening to undermine not just the American way but civilisation itself. In a commencement speech at the University of Michigan in May 1991 President George H.W. Bush criticised 'PC' as the attempt to use 'sheer force – getting their foes punished or expelled, for instance – as a substitute for the power of ideas. Throughout history, attempts to micromanage casual conversation have only incited distrust. They've invited people to look for insult in every word, gesture, action. And in their own Orwellian way, crusades that demand correct behaviour crush diversity in the name of diversity.'[27] The President said that it is not e.g. racists who threaten civilisational values, because 'racists can be reasoned with'; it is instead 'political extremists ... who roam the land, abusing the privilege of free speech, setting citizens against one another on the basis of their race or class'.[28] In the same vein, critics of Critical Race Theory claim that far from being an honest attempt at self-appraisal aimed at setting to rights the consequences of bad things that were done in the past, it is a way of deliberately loading white people with guilt and self-loathing – thereby undermining society.

As there is never smoke without fire, it would be a mistake to think that conservatives had conjured the fracas out of nothing. When campaigners meet with refusal to be heard, they raise the decibel level; when insufficient action is taken to redress wrongs in society, the degree of urgency of the problems heightens frustration and correlatively the vigour of activism. Extinction Rebellion and Just Stop Oil are contemporary examples; beyond alarmed by the danger of climate change and the perceived lethargy or indeed inactivity of those agencies with both the responsibility and competence to do something about it – chiefly governments and major international energy companies – activists take an increasingly radical stand and increasingly robust action.[29] The same phenomenon was at work in the period between the 1960s and the 1990s; the degree to which campaigns against racism and sexism had achieved some successes and met with much frustration, together with greater deployment of conceptual tools for understanding the dynamics of what resulted in the latter, had reached a point where a correlative heightening of conservative reaction to them was inevitable.

Today's 'woke wars' are a reprise of the same pattern, with much the same language, many of the same attitudes, and almost all the same explanations, still in place – yet with a major innovation: a more determined conservative backlash, in which, for example, phrases such as 'structural racism' are forbidden in undergraduate lectures at universities in 'red' states such as Florida.[30]

***

What activists in 'woke' causes want is clear enough in general terms: social justice. What this means in practical terms in the various causes is also clear enough: it is the end of discriminatory arrangements and practices, so that the effects of racism can be effaced, diversities accepted without reservation, and full equality of concern accorded to all by social, economic and governmental structures (so, for example, equality of access to and treatment by the law for all; equal pay for equal work irrespective of sex or other categorisations; in general, equality of opportunity to access social and economic goods).

CONCERNS AND COMPARISONS

Some 'wokists', frustrated by obstacles to these aims, kick harder against them, employing tactics that not only their conservative opponents but the moderates who share their aims disagree with, particularly exclusion (saliently, no-platforming and cancellation) of those they identify as perpetrating the harms they seek to have remedied. But conservative critics go further; they are vexed by the way that some institutions – universities, government departments, some companies – respond to woke aims, for a chief example by incorporating diversity, equity and inclusion (DEI) arrangements into their structures, including DEI training for staff and public commitment to its values.

The conservatives and many moderate Leftists might agree in viewing the methods of the more vigorous woke activists as a threat to free speech, and as having a punitive and vengeful character that too often exceeds demands for accountability. But in going beyond this complaint, the conservative reaction in some quarters goes to an extreme, using it to portray 'wokism' in general – now meaning not just the methods of the most radically active, but the aims of everyone on the Left, moderates and activists alike – as a conspiracy to overthrow Western civilisation itself. In particular, so they claim, it is a Marxist conspiracy. The fact that the civil rights movement and feminism both have far longer roots than Marxism does not trouble them; the ancestry of the anti-slavery movement among Quakers in the eighteenth century, the long history of Black abolitionist campaigning (think Frederick Douglass, Ira Aldridge, William Wells Brown and many others), the Enlightenment's 'rights' agenda (*vide* the

French Revolution), Mary Wollstonecraft's feminist writings of the 1790s, appear to have escaped them. In the conservatives' lexicon 'Marxism' is a dirty word, carrying with it the worst connotations of Soviet and Maoist communism as these unfolded in practice. They draw no distinction between Marx's theories about class conflict and their extension by some postmodern thinkers into theories of the effect of power differentials in society, on the one hand, and Stalinism and Maoism, on the other hand. For them, the former leads inevitably to, or just is, the latter.

It is not a tendentious point, merely a neutral one – and I make it as one who is not a Marxist – to observe that the failure to draw such a distinction exemplifies deficits in understanding both Marxist theory itself and history since the period at which Marx wrote. Just one point, of many that could be made, illustrates this: Marx's claims about the destination of the historical development of classes, which in his own era he characterised as soon to consist only of two, a bourgeoisie and a proletariat, in tension because of the economic relations between them (the tension resulting from a large part of the value created by labour being sequestered as profit by the owner of capital), can only be reached in an industrially advanced setting. Russia and China were industrially undeveloped peasant societies in which revolutions were not made by propertyless industrial workers but by small revolutionary 'vanguards', cliques, able to seize power at the centre because the putative 'masses' were too dispersed, unorganised, politically ignorant and economically depressed to do it, or do it effectively. In these dispensations the economic conditions and the endeavour to change them by means of coercive political measures failed. The Soviet experiment collapsed; the Chinese experiment assumed as many features of capitalism as could be made consistent with central political control, retaining the coercive measures. Neither the Soviet Union nor China was ever a 'Marxist' state in anything but name (and – a giveaway – a *hybridised* name at that: 'Marxist-Leninism', 'Marxist-Leninist-Mao Zedong Thought'). They were police states as the Austro-Hungarian Empire and Hitler's Third Reich were police states; they were absolutist tyrannies as Caligula's Rome or Genghis Khan's Mongolia were absolutist tyrannies. Indeed, if one were considering antecedents, the Right's own might be found here or hereabouts.

The dynamic of history worked out differently from Marx's prognostications. The industrial societies underwent political and economic developments that enlarged and strengthened a class he thought must disappear – the middle class – and at the same time generalised their economic arrangements in ways that continued to create wealth (in almost exactly the way Marx himself described) which has lifted billions of people – literally – out of poverty worldwide. But these arrangements also generate inequalities and injustices for significant minorities, felt all the more acutely by those who suffer them because of the context in which they occur, simultaneously maintaining power in sections of society reluctant to yield some of their advantages in favour of those whom the system disadvantages. These latter are those who seek remedy.

By themselves these facts, for facts they are, separate 'Marxism' from 'communism as it happened in the Soviet bloc and China' (or Cuba or eastern European countries when under Soviet domination). As has often been said, Marx was not 'a Marxist' in the pejorative sense now standard in conservative discourse. Eliding the two is a rhetorical device, a scare-mongering tactic, on which the ignorance of theories and history in the general population can rely for its effect. Thus is 'Marxism' made a bogey-word that means 'a police state in which no one is free and everyone is poor', and the 'anti-woke' warriors can ignore the points made by the various constituencies of people whom the system disadvantages, and claim that the effort to achieve remedy is a malign conspiracy to (at the limit – which 'anti-woke' warriors are quick to reach) 'overthrow Western civilisation'.

Some of the radical woke activists' methods are a gift to their opponents in this respect, for 'cancel culture', in particular, is readily compared to the repressive measures of twentieth-century communist states, based as they were on silencing – crushing – dissent. Because there is a number of causes at stake – race, sex, gender, alternative sexualities, poverty – the 'anti-woke' movement focuses attention on particular issues to distract from what is at stake in them and to amplify the effects of activism aimed at addressing them. Critical Race Theory is one, consisting in efforts to get people to become aware of major aspects of history and society and their continuing effects; another, related, effort is to raise awareness about what we say and do that, consciously or otherwise, enacts or perpetuates discrimination – DEI measures.

Here is a wholly typical example of how 'Marxism' is uncritically – indeed by conscious sleight of hand – conflated with twentieth-century communism, together with a claim that the latter's failure prompted malign conspirators to change tack by replacing 'class' with 'race':

> Rather than abandon their political project, Marxist scholars in the West simply adapted their revolutionary theory to the social and racial unrest of the 1960s. Abandoning Marx's economic dialectic of capitalists and workers, they substituted race for class and sought to create a revolutionary coalition of the dispossessed based on racial and ethnic categories.
>
> Critical race theory ... has increasingly become the default ideology in our public institutions over the past decade. It has been injected into government agencies, public school systems, teacher training programs, and corporate human-resources departments, in the form of diversity-training programs, human-resources modules, public-policy frameworks, and school curricula.
>
> Its supporters deploy a series of euphemisms to describe critical race theory, including 'equity,' 'social justice,' 'diversity and inclusion,' and 'culturally responsive teaching.' Critical race theorists, masters of language construction, realize that 'neo-Marxism' would be a hard sell. Equity, on the other hand, sounds non-threatening and is easily confused with the American principle of *equality*. But the distinction is vast and important. Indeed, critical race theorists explicitly reject equality – the principle proclaimed in the Declaration of Independence, defended in the Civil War, and codified into law

with the Fourteenth and Fifteenth Amendments, the Civil Rights Act of 1964, and the Voting Rights Act of 1965. To them, equality represents 'mere nondiscrimination' and provides 'camouflage' for white supremacy, patriarchy, and oppression.

In contrast to equality, equity as defined and promoted by critical race theorists is little more than reformulated Marxism. In the name of equity, UCLA law professor and critical race theorist Cheryl Harris has proposed suspending private property rights, seizing land and wealth, and redistributing them along racial lines. Critical race guru Ibram X. Kendi, who directs the Center for Antiracist Research at Boston University, has proposed the creation of a federal Department of Antiracism. This department would be independent of (i.e., unaccountable to) the elected branches of government, and would have the power to nullify, veto, or abolish any law at any level of government and curtail the speech of political leaders and others deemed insufficiently 'antiracist.'

One practical result of the creation of such a department would be the overthrow of capitalism, since, according to Kendi, 'In order to truly be antiracist, you also have to truly be anti-capitalist.' In other words, identity is the means; Marxism is the end.

An equity-based form of government would mean the end not only of private property but also of individual rights, equality under the law, federalism, and freedom of speech. These would be replaced by race-based redistribution of wealth, group-based rights, active discrimination, and omnipotent bureaucratic authority. Historically, the accusation of 'anti-Americanism' has been overused. But in this case, it's not a matter of interpretation: critical race theory prescribes a revolutionary program that would overturn the principles of the Declaration and destroy the remaining structure of the Constitution.[31]

This is a text in which students of rhetoric would find much to enjoy as a paradigm of polemic. For present purposes, note two things: the author's use of statements by extreme 'wokists' to discredit not just all 'wokism' but all endeavours against discrimination, and the hyperbole, if not hysteria, of the final paragraph's claim that combatting discrimination will be the 'end not only of private property but also of individual rights, equality under the law, federalism, and freedom of speech … replaced by race-based redistribution of wealth, group-based rights, active discrimination, and omnipotent bureaucratic authority', destroying the 'principles of the Declaration' and 'the Constitution'. Here hyperbole and hysteria on the Right mirror its *bêtes noires* of 'wokist' talk about 'women with penises' and 'pregnant men'. There is no recognition that, as with all things else, where there is smoke there is fire; concerns about 'white supremacy, patriarchy, and oppression' have a source, ignorable if dealing with the source is tantamount to wholesale overthrow of the American way, no middle course being possible. In the writer's view, to preserve his vision of 'Americanism' it would seem – at least it comes close to seeming – that racism, sexism, homophobia and other discriminatory attitudes, together with their practical effects on human individuals, must not be combatted.

It is true that freedom of expression, individual liberties and fair treatment are essential rights, both for individuals and the societies within which individuals can have a chance of flourishing. It is true that extreme views on left and right of the political spectrum are inimical to these rights. Both extremes engage in cancelling endeavours; the passage just quoted urges it in regard to those who wish to raise consciousness about discrimination, while more radical woke activists do it to people and institutions who are caught doing discriminatory harm, or are perceived as doing so. But it is simply wrong, and simplistic, to think that these key rights cannot be protected unless they are denied to certain groups. On the hyperbolic margins of *both* sides of the 'woke wars' this is an assumption that the more extreme activists make, destructively for the rights themselves, and for the health of society.

7

THE BOTTOM LINE

What the opponents of 'woke warriors' fail to see is that the motivation for the latter's activism comes either from personal experience of the issues at stake, or from allies' empathy with them. The allies see, as those directly affected feel, the disadvantages that discriminatory institutions, attitudes and practices impose – chiefly by denial of rights and raised barriers to accessing a range of social goods. One of the relevant social goods is being able to live according to lifestyle choices that do not violate the rights of others to do the same. What the opponents of 'wokism' see instead is the anger and hostility that its warriors feel towards those institutions, attitudes and practices, and – because the opponents benefit from these latter, and value the positive aspects in them which the warriors undervalue or ignore – defend them sometimes as indiscriminately as they accuse the warriors of doing in reverse.

The warriors' opponents indeed have interests that the warriors impugn; in addition to wishing to retain the structures that benefit them socially and economically, they typically also have an interest in upholding certain traditional or conventional norms of behaviour which they sincerely believe are right, and correlatively, perhaps, because they are disgusted by certain alternative types of behaviour, and e.g. wish to shield their children from what they regard as their malign influence (LGBTQ+ identities are chief among these). But the question is not whether their *interests* are challenged by the warriors' goals; they indeed are; it is whether their *rights* are.

If the warriors' opponents could be moved to a sufficient degree of empathy for individual circumstances of social and economic disability caused by the institutions and practices at issue, and if the warriors could understand that not everything about those institutions and practices is bad – rather the contrary: the warriors benefit from many aspects of them, which is not an *ad hominem* point but relates to the very circumstances that enable them to make their case, freedom of expression to the fore among them – then much of the heat could be removed from the debates, and more light emitted.[1] In particular, if the distinction between interests and rights is clearly made, much of that heat dissipates. Rights are non-negotiable; interests can be rationally adjusted to maximise opportunities for them to coexist.

Such a rapprochement is more than desirable, it is necessary. It involves seeing what is right in each other's cases, and remedying what is wrong in them. That takes work. It is a demand for intellectual honesty. It certainly requires modification of aspects of the institutions and practices at issue, and it requires the 'woke warriors' to recognise the harm that aspects of their activism can do, to society and particularly to individuals on both sides. The harm is something the warriors desire for individuals whom they regard as baleful, but the result is that they do not merely punish the latter but damage too many others on the way. A particularly vexing example is the transgender issue.[2] There are sincere people on both sides of this debate. In defending the rights of transgender people, warriors commit themselves to positions on matters of biology, gender, sexuality, self-identification and choice at least some of which prompt those who disagree into becoming entrenched on their own side, insisting ever more strongly on binaries that impugn the rights of those whom the warriors champion. The realities on both sides are lost to view in the smoke of battle, and the very fact that it is a battle and not a discourse of mutual recognition creates victims on both sides, as battles always do.

As in a domestic quarrel that grows more heated with mounting accusations and counter-accusations, so division increases. Much disappears down the gap between. One of these things is the health of the society itself. An especially dismaying feature is the way that 'woke wars' are politicised, in the sense of becoming identified with 'Left' and 'Right' labels. The very terms are red rags.

Yet a dispassionate examination of some of the views held by participants does not suggest that the labels readily fit them, especially when the views are nuanced. Occupants of less radical positions on the spectrum are branded by occupants of more radical positions thus: centre-Right are merely Right, centre-Left are wishy-washy and useless to any cause, other than (says the Right) in being enabling fellow-travellers of the further Left. 'Liberal' (not 'libertarian', a further-Right position), 'progressive' and 'social democratic' are not good enough for the ultras on the woke side, despite sharing almost every aim with them apart from methodology. 'Liberal', 'progressive' and 'social democratic' are centre-Left or moderate-Left positions (though in the US 'liberal' has come to be caricatured almost as 'tyrannically communist with bloodied teeth', just as the entire Right has come to be viewed by most on the Left as no better than Fascists with equally bloodied teeth). It is precisely the disagreement over methodology that makes the ultras disparage the moderate Left. It is also the reason why some – who until the 'woke wars' became vocally and conceptually shrill would self-describe as 'Left' – have distanced themselves from the ultras, labelling them *radical or ultra Left*' and disavowing alliance with their methods and in some cases even their framing of the problems at issue. An effect of these further divisions in an already historically fragmented Left is to widen the divide in the political spectrum overall, by pushing the Right further rightward in reaction, while weakening the case for moderate options on the Left, not least by giving the Right weapons to oppose all progressive aims by painting the whole Left in the colours of its ultras.

In one sense the ultras have reason to disparage the moderate Left, because the Right, already in possession of so many advantages, have a genius for exploiting any gradualism on the part of their opponents as a way of continuing, even entrenching, their advantages. The ultras know this. The logic of their view has been played out in history: the logic is that the most emphatic way to defeat the Right is by revolution.

But history teaches that almost all revolutions, their objectives rarely achieved by those who in a burst of idealism started them, are disastrous methods. The Terror that followed the French Revolution, the Stalinism that followed the Russian Revolution, are examples of what happens when, as the promise of the revolution fails, its putative gains can only be preserved by enforcements even worse, or at best no better, than what it replaced. More recent examples teach the same lesson: the demonstrators in Cairo's Tahrir Square in January 2011, bringing down President Hosni Mubarak, did not thereby create a better society.[3] First an Islamist government under Mohamed Morsi, then its displacement by Abdel Fattah el-Sisi, saw to that. Neither of the successor administrations to Mubarak realised the ambitions that many of the demonstrators in Tahrir Square risked their lives for. If anything, with over 60,000 political prisoners in Egypt's jails today, things are worse.

Revolution as the most *emphatic* way to defeat any oppressive regime of whatever political colour tends to be the most temporary way, and is therefore not the *definitive* way. Matters have to be viewed through a quite different lens instead, by recognising that every society, save for those given the artificial appearance of being otherwise through coercion and lies, is a variegated fabric of many minorities and individuals. Temporary and artificial majorities are created by coalitions of minorities over particular issues at particular times, such as at elections in places that have them. Otherwise the society is a product of continual negotiation, a series of balancing acts, imbalances being the norm until by one or another means they are corrected or over-corrected. What counts as equilibrium is itself a matter of negotiation. Survey the history of any 'advanced liberal democracy' in the period since 1945 and this pattern is manifest. Given the character of society as a fabric of minorities, this is inevitable. The negotiations that produce the overall character of a society at any point in its history do not concern only its politics and government, but all its institutions and practices. The negotiations take the form of public debate, campaigns, the vectoring of many interests into overall directions of travel. Individual influencers on this topic or that, and certainly in politics, tend to have a disproportionate effect on such vectoring, not least because many if not most people wait to be told, or have suggested to them, what they should think. This is where bias, misinformation and polemic do much work – one is tempted to say, most of the work. The temptation comes from the undeniable fact that all points of view, save those that come from dispassionate expertise – a rare element in the public conversation, getting too little exposure or at least attention in mainstream and social media – tend to be put tendentiously; this is indeed the very DNA of political 'debate', which is not debate so much as charge and counter-charge, clashes of opinion, public relations competitions. The holder of a point of view wishes to have others accept it because of course he thinks he is right. All those of us who have definite views about a matter have succumbed to the urge to accentuate the positive and downplay the negative rather than seeking compromise. Alas.

THE BOTTOM LINE

The task of recognising where compromises are not appropriate, and identifying those where they will help achieve productive near-equilibrium, demands really good thinking. There can and should be no compromise on racism, sexism, slavery, homophobia, and systemic structures that result in the accumulation of vastly disproportionate holdings of power and wealth *at the expense* of majorities of people. No middle course exists for these things. And that is because *individuals* suffer harms as a result of them, and the aggregate effect of these harms is to constrain them in groups that, as groups, reflect the individual effects. There is no halfway house on slavery or executing gay people. At the same time, there is nothing wrong with anyone being rich, even very rich, providing that his being so is not the result of deliberately loading the system against others in order that he can be so. Let anyone be as rich as they like providing that no one is poor, struggling to feed her children, living anxiously from day to day, hand to mouth, in uncomfortable or wretched conditions. The fact is that there are people who are rich *because* there are people who live like that. Proof is provided by any system of taxation so designed that it yields too little to provide basic decency and security for those at the bottom of the pile because by choice it leaves large amounts in the hands of the already well-off. And it is the already well-off who have a greater influence on this choice being made. Generalise this point *mutatis mutandis* to other issues over which 'woke wars' rage, and one begins to see that the implicit assumption in them, viz. that they are zero-sum games, is false. This is a point that tells against the warriors on both sides.

Schematically – using simplified terms of conflict theory, which nevertheless capture something suggestive – the factors that lead to the kind of situation that the 'woke wars' exemplify are these: the evolution of social and economic arrangements produces an at least eventually noticeable difference between those who are relatively Up and those who are relatively Down in how much they benefit from or are disadvantaged by the arrangements. These are relative positions; there is a great difference between what 'poverty' means in the Global South and the Global North respectively. Self-interest and self-protection work better for the Up because they have better means to express the first and achieve the second. (Self-interest, not irrelevantly, is sometimes hard to tell apart from selfishness.) As a result the arrangements are loaded – in some places more, in others less – against the Down and their efforts to rebalance the loading. Despite the tactic, and its modern analogues, of Rome's 'bread and circus' distractions from the arrangement's inequities, the Down and those who sympathise with them, being or having become aware of ('woke' to) the reasons why they are Down, are or become yet more frustrated. Frustration leads to anger and resentment, and both by their nature emotionalise the terms in which matters are framed; at the extreme of this process, the Down assume, and/or their champions endow them with, the saintliness of victimhood and possession of the truth. At the same time they endow the Up with all manner of wicked schemes and intentions. In response the Up, now that disbursing more crumbs from the table has not worked, respond by seeing Marxist plots and threats to civilisation in the now-angry Down activism. There is enough truth in the Down's view of the Up's activities and the Up's view of what the Down are calling in aid for their efforts, to make the opposition between them fraught.

The suggestion that the impasse would be resolved by upping the Down rather than downing the Up – which on this way of framing the matter has a considerable measure of good sense in it – does not persuade either party because the Up do not believe that upping the Down would leave them as Up as before, and for some Down their resentment of the Up is not appeased by leaving them Up – for after all, the *relative* Upness and Downness in question might not change enough, from those Down's point of view, even if they achieve a considerable upping; the Up must accept an adjustment that meets the Down's sense that they, the Up, have had it good at their, the Down's, expense, in a way that justice requires.

This schematic portrayal of matters is the crudest of first passes, because it leaves out so much that needs examination. One, mentioned to be left aside, is that the values of consumer society play a large part in perceptions of Upness and Downness. How big your house is, what furniture and clothes you have, what car or cars you own, where you go on holiday and how often, where you educate your offspring – in general: what is available to you from the glittering array of consumables available after basic needs are met – play a part in the *perceptual* relativity of Upness and Downness.

But they are beside the point in what is really at stake, which is whether individuals' rights are respected, or alternatively compromised or denied, by the way the arrangements work. In a situation in which they are so structured as to impose barriers against an individual's aspiration to uncompromised exercise of her rights, while advantaging others to realise the same aspiration, the relativity in *this* crucial respect of the difference between Up and Down is illegitimate. In a situation in which individuals have equally unfettered opportunity to build on what their rights entitle them to, if some become more Up than others through harder work, more talent or greater luck (and thereby have the bigger house, the smarter car, etc. etc.), there can be no complaint. One might be jealous of someone more Up than oneself, if one cares about the sorts of things he has and does, but if his possession of them is not a function, however indirectly, of one's being denied *by the arrangements* the opportunity to be as Up as he is, one's feeling jealous (as with feeling offended) is not a justification for tearing him down.

Yet this still leaves out a point, an equally crucial point: that what the Downness of the Down consists in has to be understood for what it is, to see what upping it involves. Consider a person confined for life to a wheelchair. As a person, she has the right to access public buildings, to an education, to privacy, to equal treatment before the law, and the rest of her rights. And she has an *equalising* right to social disbursements and arrangements that address the barriers to exercising these other rights – which means, to what endows her with equality in respect of them, including requirements on public buildings to provide disabled access, toilets, and whatever else is necessary. Providing these – providing what makes possible the full recognition of the rights of all – carries a cost. Up reluctance to adjusting the arrangements (e.g. through relevant levels of taxation) inhibits, compromises or undermines making such provision. Financial cost is not the only one; the cost of removing psychological and social reluctances can be high too – these feed into the practical reluctance, and make it much more difficult to overcome.

One of the social goods already mentioned is being able to live according to lifestyle choices that do not violate the rights of others to do the same. This applies to choosing to love and have a family life with members of the same sex or gender, to engage in consensual sexual activity with persons having the same tastes, to live in accordance with gender characteristics that feel right for oneself, to be treated as a human being and not a member of a group if a group identity is not what one chooses as the principal determiner of how one's presence in society is responded to – in short, to be granted one's human rights. One's possession of rights places obligations on others to respect them; but no exercise of one's own rights can be allowed to violate another's rights, otherwise the rights project is defeated for all. Affecting the *interests* of others by the exercise of one's rights is another matter; one is entitled to do so in order to achieve the exercise of one's rights, though by no means all such conflicts between rights and interests are irresolvable. And there is the thought that in civil society how this is done should, to the extent possible, respect the 'civil' in that phrase.

The uncomfortable truth for Ups to accept is that contemporary social and political arrangements in what are said to be 'advanced democratic economies' do indeed infringe rights by loading the dice against many. The uncomfortable truth for Downs to accept is that Ups have rights. Another uncomfortable truth for Ups is that their interests are not rights. Another uncomfortable truth for Downs is that equality of concern, equality before the law, equality of inherent human dignity, equality of rights to life, privacy, opinion, expression and education, do not either individually or collectively mean 'a right to equality *as such*' – that is, the same amount of everything as everyone else. 'Equal pay for equal work', yes; 'equal e.g. size house for everyone', no – because one person might have a partner and ten children while another lives alone. Each member of the big family and the solitary have an equal right to a decent home, but the solitary does not have a right to claim as big a house as the family *because* of the family's house's size. This kind of thought-elision operates too often in appeals to rights, misjudging their purport.

'Freedom of expression' emerges as a key matter. Note 'freedom of expression' is more accurate than just 'freedom of speech', because it includes not just speech (*viva voce* or written) but plastic art, cartoons, theatre performances, dance, advertisements, marches and demonstrations, political parties, indeed anything that does or can assert, display or embody a standpoint.

The Right, who once had a near-monopoly of free expression because they controlled most of the means for it, thus muting or even silencing voices of complaint by victims of discrimination – and so not much different in practice from the way explicitly oppressive regimes silenced whole societies – now object, rightly, to radical woke activist silencings through no-platforming and cancellation. The radical wokist silencing is the product of wishing to have the voices of the discriminated-against heard, those voices historically drowned by the massive roar of the mainstream machine which enacted that discrimination. Thus, radical wokist silencing consists in a cry to 'Shut up and listen!' Whereas the demand to listen to repressed voices is right, the question is whether a reverse silencing is the right way to demand it.

Why 'rightly' in connection with conservative charges against aspects of radical woke activism? Because freedom of expression is fundamental to all rights. Without freedom of expression there cannot be law under which accusation and defence are possible. Without freedom of expression there cannot be education worth the name, if information cannot be communicated, and if ideas and points of view cannot be expressed, examined and criticised. Without freedom of expression there cannot be a democratic political process in which policies can be proposed and likewise examined and criticised. Without freedom of expression there cannot be a free press. Without freedom of expression there cannot be art and literature worth their names. Without freedom of expression there cannot be individual choices of lifestyle (which respect others' right in the same regard; that is, *their* right to freedom of expression). Without freedom of expression one cannot campaign for social justice. Without freedom of expression, in short, one cannot lay claim to, and exercise, any of one's rights, or try to change society for the better. It is therefore fundamental.

But 'fundamental' does not mean 'absolute'. There are justified cases in which it can be qualified; already mentioned is e.g. the need in wartime to censor the press lest an enemy garner important information. There is the familiar case in which irresponsible use of the freedom can cause harm – shouting 'Fire!' in a crowded theatre when there is no fire is the standard example. This prompts the question: When is free expression 'irresponsible'? The answer has to be given case by case, and has to have a justification that can withstand severe scrutiny.

As pertinent as the 'when' question is the 'how' question: How should one apply one's right to freedom of expression? Inflammatory rhetoric, abuse, misinformation, *ad hominem* attacks and vilification, spite, cruelty and hatred are licensed by freedom of expression, but pervert it. They hurt individuals and damage society. A civilised person will eschew such behaviour. But that does not rule out robust, plain-spoken, well-informed, well-organised and well-directed assertion of views or criticism of opposing views. This is in any case far more effective than inflamed rhetoric and abuse, and far more constructive. To see someone whose views you strongly oppose wither to defeat under the evidence and arguments you produce is not merely infinitely more satisfying than hurling invectives at him, which serves only to entrench him in his position and invites abuse back, but has a greater chance of winning others to your cause and to advancing the good you wish to see flourish.

Freedom of expression is a right; right ways of exercising it matter for protection of the right itself. To defeat an opponent requires knowing thoroughly what his position is – so it serves you that he exercises his freedom of expression – and being able to distinguish whether there is anything in it that is justified or at least explicable, not just what is wrong with it. That correlatively requires understanding the strengths and weaknesses of one's own position, and the degree to which one's emotional commitments colour, perhaps obscure, the weaknesses in it.

The problem faced by minorities who suffer under social and economic discrimination is how to get their point across – and acted upon – given how much the dice are loaded against them. The frustration they feel explains, whether or not it justifies, why they shout and shoulder-charge the doors locked against them. On the other side, their opponents' refusal to listen exacerbates matters; conservatives who become hysterical about the 'threat to civilisation' from the frustrations they themselves cause have their portion of blame.

Campaigners for social justice have much to gain from taking Aristotle's point about anger: 'to be angry with the right person, in the right degree, at the right time, for the right purpose'. That is not easy, but necessary. In response campaigners can say that those with their hands on the levers of privilege never let go voluntarily, that such advances as have been made against discrimination were forcibly wrested from the discriminators; witness the civil rights activism of the 1960s, the arduous struggles by feminism to gain what has so far been gained. What is true about this is that collective action is powerful; what happened in the streets and squares of Gdańsk in Poland and Prague in Czechoslovakia in 1989 – in the latter, tens of thousands gathered peacefully night after night in Wenceslas Square until the regime fell; the 'Velvet Revolution' – is an illustration. Police brutality against civil rights marches in the US and against gay people in Moscow, the army crushing (literally) students in Beijing's Tiananmen Square, and too many other instances besides, tell against an over-optimistic assumption that such demonstration of claim works.[4] But *ab esse ad posse* – 'anything actual is possible' – meaning: peaceful and well-organised collective action has worked, which shows that it can work.

But an essential element in the success of the movements in Czechoslovakia and elsewhere was that the regimes had no arguments, and the opposition to them had united around an irrefutable case, in Czechoslovakia articulated with clarity and cogency by Václav Havel. It is striking that, to the extent that movements of liberation in the second half of the twentieth century relied on having a focus and leader in charismatic individuals such as Martin Luther King, Lech Wałęsa, Václav Havel and Nelson Mandela, none of these men advocated violence, and after succeeding none of the latter three encouraged revenge. They did not even engage in 'violent *speech*' – recalling that in the conceptual lexicon of radical activists on the woke side, discriminatory speech is regarded as a form of violence, to be countered by an opposing reaction of silencing it.

The 'woke wars' case is not exactly comparable to the instances just cited, because whereas the collapsing communist regimes had no arguments, the opponents of the 'wokists' do have some – not arguments providing any justification for discrimination, but arguments about some of the radical activists' methods. The Right sees the methods as 'threatening civilisation' – meaning, their privileges – but moderate allies of the radical activists see them as threatening to self-defeat the causes at issue.

***

The idea of engaging the processes of public policy, and working to direct them towards addressing what is at issue in social justice campaigns, is central to moderate wokism. Arguably, the adoption of Critical Race Theory in schools in the US, much countered in conservative states and (at the instigation of 'anti-wokist' activism) in federal policy under Donald Trump, is an example of how progress can be achieved, succeeding in getting practical implementation of programmes that scrutinised the causes and nature of racism. Another, associated, example is the widespread adoption of DEI programmes in institutions and companies. But radical woke activists are sceptical about this strategy, a scepticism that – for some – translates into a belief that democracy, which has not sufficiently delivered solutions to the problems that concern them, is incapable of doing so. One reason these sceptics might give is that democracy (putatively) expresses the will of the majority, and the majority of people are prejudiced. The real reason is rather different, though widespread prejudices indeed enter the picture. It can be explained as follows.

The US and about fifty other states around the world have a system of democracy based on the 'Westminster Model', the electoral, parliamentary and governmental model derived originally from England and adapted under various names and arrangements.[5] In the nineteenth century and afterwards all of them saw an incremental widening of the franchise, and in response a tightening and formalisation of party-political organisation. Since almost all the Westminster-derived systems employ electoral systems and party organisations that strongly favour two-party outcomes, the result is that government alternates, when it does, between two broad political factions with contrasting ideas about public policy directions. James Madison, in the tenth Federalist Paper, warned against 'factionalism' – party politics – because when it obtains and one of the factions secures power, it will apply its power in ways that advantage its supporters to the possible disadvantage of others.[6] What he warned against has come to pass, potentiated by party discipline and the binary all-or-nothing choice that the voting public is obliged to make.

Party discipline (together with the imperatives of political careerism among the party's members) results in representatives 'of the people' in fact being representatives not of the people but 'of the party line'. In turn, the party depends upon its constituency of support in part of the electorate for continued tenure of power, which is where prejudices enter the picture; a party in government, wishing to be re-elected next time round, will be reluctant to institute policies counter to the prejudices of those who support it, or will act in ways that appease those prejudices, and anyway will act in ways that advantage its supporters in order to retain their support. In two-party systems, government might be 'government *of* the people' but is not 'government *for* the people' where 'people' means everyone; instead, it is 'government *for the people who support it*'.

This system is not well suited to societies whose populations are relatively numerous and diverse. All societies are congeries of minorities, and minorities are congeries of individuals; there is no such thing as 'a majority' as such, other than as a temporary coalition of minorities created by a particular circumstance such as an election or referendum. In countries that have proportional representation systems, such as most member states of the European Union, the diversity of interests, desires and needs of the various minorities have a better chance of some representation in the legislature, which in turn, when an executive is formed from it, has to reach agreements and make arrangements in which matters of importance to minorities are taken into account. No system is perfect, far from it, but in these systems the possibility of minority interests being considered is greater than in two-party systems, and the possibility of getting those interests noted and acted upon is correlatively greater.

In two-party systems *government* is, in effect, *politics*. Debates in the legislature are political clashes, government decisions are politically shaped, the government has one eye on re-election in deciding what to do. How policy is decided upon and presented is attentive to its public relations impact. The nature of politics, already distrusted by the electorate because of these factors, makes it hard for a government to take necessary but at times unpopular decisions that are in the interests of all.

DISCRIMINATIONS

In short, the process of government has been hijacked by party politics, especially in Westminster-derived polities, and makes it insensitive to views and interests of some minorities. Getting those interests noticed and acted upon, even when fully justified, is hard, takes time and effort, and frequently fails. For those suffering the effects of discriminatory structures and practices, let alone attitudes, in society, this is vexing and frustrating. It is a generalisation, but one which can be supported in broad strokes by a survey of European societies such as the Pew report on European attitudes to moral issues,[7] that apart from the most serious of all the problems that concern those on the woke side, viz. racism, which is endemic everywhere, attitudes towards alternative sexualities (towards sex and drugs in general) and towards women and transgender people tend to be more relaxed. This is connected to the way the political arrangements allow a greater range of interests to find a voice and achieve a platform.[8]

No doubt it is further frustrating to be told that achieving progress in one direction requires making progress in another, different, direction. But obviously enough, reforming political structures is a key part of reforming social and economic conditions, not necessarily (as conservatives fear) by wholesale revolution, still less by introducing changes in the direction of greater and more widespread repressions, but for example by a proportional system of voting in elections in place of the two-party 'first-past-the-post' system, which entrenches binaries and is sclerotically resistant to systemic changes.

How 'the people' are represented is one major part of any system in which the diversity of interests in society can be optimally addressed. Another is the constitutional order itself, specifying the powers and duties of elected and appointed government officials. These officials are servants of the people – you would think, observing presidents and prime ministers, that by contrast they think themselves the people's bosses – and a constitution should set out what is expected of them and what the limits on the exercise of their office are.[9]

Together, the electoral system and the constitution are the structural part of democracy. The other part is the people themselves. Ideally, voters in a democracy should be informed, thoughtful, willing to share the burdens as well as the benefits of making society and economy work to the best advantage of all. 'Ideally'; obviously this is a utopian hope; it was indeed the basis of Plato's complaint against democracy, in the eighth book of his *Republic*, that he thought 'the people' ill-informed, self-interested, short-termist, quarrelsome – in short, a mob – who could not be relied upon to take sensible decisions. Education for a maturely rational society is one corrective for this cynical – or realistic – view of 'the people', but education has increasingly become something different from a mission to encourage examination of ideas, and instead focuses on preparing high school and college graduates for service to the economy – thus, not *education* in the true sense, but *training*; not inviting critical thought about values and possibilities, knowledge of other ways of thinking, other times, other perspectives – as provided by history, literature and philosophy – but instead technical competence with computers and business studies, chemistry, electronics, accountancy, economics, law: all necessary in a technological age driven by commerce, yes, but lacking the perspective that the humanities bring to the possibility of individually enriched and socially-aware lives capable of mature, contributory, constructively critical membership of society.

In short, the way 'democracy' – especially in the Anglophone world, but not restricted to it – has transmogrified into 'party politics' explains much about the entrenchment of discriminatory structures in society. This in turn explains frustration, and the bitterness of divides over the issues that wokism addresses. By their nature conservatives are committed to preserving the structures that serve them, and they regard attempts to remodel these structures as a threat. Resistance increases the radicalism of their opponents. Wokism is an expression not only of the discrimination under which minorities suffer, but of the sheer difficulty they experience in securing redress. Every advance they make raises the possibility of further advances – but this very fact hardens conservative resistance. This is a perpetual dialectic, but there are critical moments in the evolution of societies when the friction produced reaches a particularly high point. The 'woke wars' are one such point.

Times of difficulty are times of opportunity. When things break down, the chance of building anew offers itself. Times of difficulty can thus be times of hope. Whether they are so depends on whether we make them so: the future is not fixed, it waits to be created. At issue in the 'woke wars' is the idea of a just – a *fair* and *inclusive* – society. It will not be achieved by deepening divides and increasing hostilities. How, then, is it to be done? Some suggestions, and the realities they involve, are offered in the next chapter.

8

ROADS TO *PAX HUMANA*

A bird's-eye view of social changes in the Anglophone and western European world in the period since 1945 yields a remarkable picture. Even against a background of major geopolitical and economic change – listed earlier: the Cold War, the end of colonialism, the collapse of the Soviet Union, the rise of China, with a continuous seething of conflicts and upheavals in many parts of the world – social change, in the West at least, looks just as dramatic. Those alive throughout this era saw remarkable advances on several fronts: civil rights, women's causes and greater LGBTQ+ acceptance chief among them. Already mentioned is the fact that these advances empowered those who made them to seek more at each stage, with some notable successes. The decriminalisation of homosexuality, the greatly improved relative position of women in socio-economic terms together with the degree of control they have over their reproductive choices, and the removal of at least some racist barriers towards a more inclusive society, must be acknowledged.

DISCRIMINATIONS

But it goes without saying that the journey towards a non-discriminatory social order is far from over, the advances themselves revealing how much remains to be done. As layers of discrimination are peeled away, so deeper layers are exposed. Slavery and subsequent apartheid – Jim Crow in the US – might be over, but racism in both systemic and subtler forms persists. Overt sexism might have diminished, but structural barriers to equality for women in public and economic life continue. LGBTQ+ people enjoy acceptance in Western cosmopolitan settings, but are still regarded askance in smaller urban and rural conservative areas, especially of the US, and met with hostility and persecution in many countries outside the West.

In more recent decades two causes have joined the palette of concerns: the climate crisis, and more latterly still, gender identity. The urgency of the climate issue has prompted commensurate forms of activism.[1] It might be said that these two causes lie at different ends of a spectrum; climate change poses an extreme and imminent threat to all humanity and the planet, while transgender debates – rightly of great concern to individuals involved – are (so some unsympathetic critics say) a niche concern, and one where the focus of activism is (again as the unsympathetic say) misplaced, aiming as it does to change language and perceptions about conventional binaries and 'biological realities'. The bitterness of controversy tends to be far greater in matters of the latter scope than in those of global concern. And arguably, where response to the climate crisis should itself be global, with the world co-operating on a war footing to limit or at least mitigate the disastrous effects of climate warming, the transgender issue should be much more easily resolvable with generosity and acceptance, for it involves important realities for the individuals involved, and the only barrier to accommodating those realities is the surmountable one of cost, the cost of accommodating sensitivities on all sides – for example, by providing spaces (toilets, changing rooms, prisons) where no one is going to feel upset or threatened in the way that lies at the centre of the debate's more acerbic reaches.[2]

The continuation of racist, sexist and other forms of discrimination is the source of woke endeavours to combat them; the difficulty these endeavours face explains the frustration that prompts some wokists to more extreme measures. 'Anti-wokists' lump all wokists together, being undiscriminating – ironically – about the causes at issue. It is after all useful to have an excuse for delaying environmental action if environment activists can be aggregated with Me Too, Black Lives Matter and transgender activists, and conservatives can point to *outré* examples of wokism in some areas in order to discredit all areas of active concern. If for no other reason, activists in the various causes would do well to observe Aristotle's Principle about being angry in the right way for the right reasons in the right contexts. In particular, attention has to be paid to the crucial matter of freedom of expression, which all activists need and yet which some activists deny to opponents, thus gifting conservatives a potent weapon in response.

The nub of the issue is this: the aims of wokism are right, but some of the methods are questionable and in two significant respects – no-platforming and cancelling – too often especially so. Both no-platforming and cancelling are attacks on freedom of expression. But cancelling is the more extreme measure; it is othering, demonising, silencing, excluding. It can feel, and in fact really can be, wholly justified in the case of very disagreeable people who have a malign record of doing harm – and after all, society as a whole cancels individuals in appropriate cases, as when it imprisons criminals. But there is a large difference between cancellation as the outcome of a due process and as the outcome of an informal social media process. Cancelling is a spectrum, its commonest expression in the 'woke wars' a collective social-media-disseminated repudiation of an individual for some real or perceived malfeasance, which can mean loss of reputation and even livelihood for the targeted person. That is no light thing. The spectrum has a grim far end where the multitudinous ghosts of the Holocaust cluster in mute warning. Note that trial by social media denies the target's right to a fair trial, because the accusers and prosecutors are also the judges, and a punishment such as loss of livelihood or even just loss of reputation is a very serious one which might be disproportionate to the offence.

Matters are compounded if institutions – businesses, universities – do not allow due process in cases where an employee has become the subject of a social media trial. Recall the example of Osama bin Laden in chapter 1: few less palatable subjects for due consideration from a human rights perspective can be imagined, but the point is not bin Laden but the institution – in this case the United States of America itself – and how it behaves. Matters are also compounded if the punishment in woke contexts is such that there is no way back, no rehabilitation, no second chances, for the target of a social media trial; which makes it a life sentence, which is at least disproportionate in some cases, and risks the injustice that 'mob justice' is too apt to administer. We look with horror at lynchings and at crowds beating to death a hated individual; the idea of due process at law is specific to rescuing anyone, guilty or not, from the frenzied injustice of the mob. Trial by social media is mob injustice, even of the palpably guilty.

Consider the concept of freedom of expression again, and note what it assumes. It assumes that there will be a diversity of views in most communities, and demands acceptance of the fact that people will not always agree about everything. This is what underlies the requirement for mutual recognition of the right to free expression: the right to disagree, the right to have a view and to express it, the right to be heard, the right to a place in the debate (which is, in effect: a right to participation in society). Some will find the views of others abhorrent. They will find the application of those views in practice unacceptable. When power lies with the views and their application, and when there are victims of the latter, there is concern, even outrage – and with it the appropriate desire to remedy matters. Here is where the question of method enters. Frustration with incremental reform is understandable. At times, more confrontational methods have been successful: marches, demonstrations, strikes. At other times the backlash provoked by confrontational methods has set the cause back. Remembering that real individuals suffer the real effects of injustice and discrimination suggests that applying methods that provoke setbacks is not the right way to go.

DISCRIMINATIONS

What is the right way? Let us adopt again the method of stating an ideal, and then looking at the work required to approach it as closely as possible. Recall the point that all societies are congeries of minorities and individuals, with various outlooks, interests and needs sometimes shared by some of the minorities with each other, and sometimes differing and even competing. This is what 'diversity' means. Accordingly, the ideal is not *unity* – which could be achieved only by effacing differences, enforcing conformity, excluding the diverse – but *harmony*, in which all parties, accepting the diversities among them, get along in mutual tolerance, granting each other the space to be themselves and to live their choices, under one major constraint: that each respects the other's *rights* – which means that the exercise of one's rights must take into account others' exercise of their rights.

The name for a situation of social harmony is *convivencia*, which ought to be the primary target of justice endeavours. The term itself should be constantly in our mouths as we debate and negotiate the conditions of socio-economic life, as denoting the idea – the ideal – of diverse communities living together positively. As mentioned earlier, the source of the term *'convivencia'* is said to be the peaceful coexistence between Muslims, Jews and Christians in Spain between the eighth and fifteenth centuries CE.[3] Whether or not Andalusian *convivencia* is a myth – or merely just 'more complicated' than the rosy view of it suggests, which of course is likely – the idea is an immensely attractive one.

So: the desideratum is *convivencia*; the slogan for it is *not unity but harmony* – and the clincher is that *harmony is achieved by mutual respect for rights.*

In turn this requires having a clear awareness of the distinction between *rights* and *interests*, for whereas respecting others' interests so long as they do not diminish or conflict with one's own is the obvious course, it may and often enough does happen that interests conflict. When they do, resolutions have to be found on a case-by-case basis. Often enough a clash of interests is not easily resolved, and then one or both parties lose out. Again on a case-by-case basis, this is not invariably a matter of injustice; if one shoe shop loses customers because a neighbouring shoe shop has more effective sales personnel, no injustice is involved in one interest out-competing another.

But obviously enough there are cases where conflicts involve injustice; these are the cases where the *rights* of the losing party have been subordinated to the *interests* of the winning party. This is precisely the situation in racism, sexism, and other forms of discrimination. And this is where the work of achieving, or getting as close as possible to, *convivencia* has to be done.

A natural thought is that getting along peacefully with neighbours involves compromise. That is true enough for mundane cases: keeping your music down late at night, agreeing on the boundary line between your own and next door's garden. But there is no compromise over discrimination – over racism, sexism and homophobia. Once again, the *rights* versus *interests* distinction is key. Compromise is always possible and often necessary over interests; it does not apply to rights. Recall that the principle underlying a specification of rights is that they open a space around an individual that allows her to make choices relevant to her interests and needs – privacy, protection by the law, entitlement to her beliefs, and the rest – subject only to her respecting the rights of others to the same. This is where compromises relating to her *interests* come into play, and where it is in her interests to waive a right (as with privacy, in becoming intimate with another person) her doing so is not an abandonment of the right *per se* but of a choice not to exercise it in a particular case.

In interpersonal relationships we make a space for others, accepting the differences between us that the space allows for. We cannot expect everyone to like who we are or what we do or choose, nor always to make allowances for us, especially our failures. But we can expect our rights to be observed, and – a separate matter – we can reasonably expect to be treated with good manners. All of this applies to how we regard others and how we treat them; we do not have to like everyone we meet or think favourably of their behaviour and choices, but we have to respect their rights, and we do well – to ourselves as to them – if we are good-mannered. This is not a trivial point; reflection will suggest that, fundamentally, morality is a matter of good manners – of treating others with consideration unless they forfeit our consideration; and even then not descending to their level of behaviour in response.[4]

Diversity is not the same as division. A diverse society can be harmonious if everyone's rights are respected and differences (of interests and needs) are accommodated accordingly.

But inevitably there will be debate, and disagreements, over particular issues, and over larger questions of the direction of socio-economic travel; the latter in particular is the province of politics. It is undesirable for politics to replace government, once an administration is formed as the outcome of the society's political conversation with itself, but the conversation itself is an essential preliminary to government.[5] A key point here is offered by John Stuart Mill: 'Only through diversity of opinion is there, in the existing state of the human intellect, a chance of fair play to all sides of the truth'; differences of view, and debate about them, is a good which should be encouraged – always subject to respect for the rights of others.[6] Democracy is noisy; tyrannies impose silence. The downside is that vigorous debate has a tendency to degenerate into bitterness when the parties to it are heavily invested in their views and anxious to have them prevail, for then emotion enters and antipathies increase. When people are suffering harms through discrimination – being othered, excluded, denied, treated unjustly – the investment of concern is as great as it is sincere, and frustration of efforts to remedy matters explains the bitterness. The work of putting wrongs right without creating greater harms is very hard, but it has to be done.

At the simplest level of explanation for discriminatory behaviour one finds two things: prejudice and self-interest. Both have explanations (not excuses) in what are plausibly evolutionary terms. Prejudice draws on the tribal instincts that promote bonds with kin but at the same time impel 'othering' of strangers and people who are different and unfamiliar. Self-interest has its roots in self-preservation, and is not necessarily malign; it becomes so when it takes the forms of selfishness and greed, which it often enough does. A combination of self-interest with the othering instinct, and an assumption that the othered are or could be a threat in some way to one's self-interest, is the volatile mixture that underlies much of the suspicion and avoidance, even hostility, that marks relations between groups and whole peoples. When *interests* clash, an almost invariable immediate effect is diminished sympathy for others' *rights*.

Prejudices – literally: pre-judging the character and worth of another; and in the forms of racism and sexism on the indiscriminately general grounds of a single salient (supposed) fact, viz., a perceived group identity – involve an automatic diminished sympathy for the rights of the others in the target group. Prejudices might be formed by experience, as when an encounter with some representatives of a group (say, the people of a country one is visiting) goes badly and one generalises from it to an ill view of the group as a whole. It goes without saying that generalisation of this kind is unjustified, still less so the prejudice founded on it; but it happens frequently. One hears such remarks as 'I don't like the French' or 'I don't like Muslims', and the sheer absurdity, not to say stupidity, of such avowals is breathtaking.

Even worse, however, is prejudice inherited through membership of a group, which is standardly the case with racism and sexism. The dislike felt by prejudiced people for an entire 'race' as well as individual members of it, or for all women (or all men) similarly, is not based on grounds from which it is derived as an inference, but because it is a sentiment imbibed from the attitudes and language of one's community. One of the reasons that prejudice is hard to overcome is that it is difficult to reason people out of views they were not reasoned into – and prejudice is an emotion-based, emotion-derived reflex. A peculiarity of it is that people can continue to be prejudiced in this way despite knowing and liking individual members of the group towards which they are prejudiced.

Indeed prejudice can be anti-group without being actively anti-individual. A person by any standards racist in attitudes towards (say) African Americans collectively might get on perfectly well with individuals encountered. This might be how a form of *convivencia* in fact plays out in contemporary society, if it achieves the practical end of social justice thereby. On this view, it would not matter what people's private feelings are so long as they always act with express respect for others' rights. But the problem with this is how it manifests *structurally* – in assumptions that (say) police officers make on seeing a group of black youths gathered in a vacant lot, in a human resources manager sifting through application forms and making assumptions on the basis of names – or in the case of sexism, in the way the working week is organised prejudicially to people, almost always women, who have commitments as carers of children or elderly relatives alongside their employment. These structural manifestations of prejudice are less obvious to all but their victims than the earlier and more explicit versions from which they derive; but are no less real.

It would, however, be a mistake to rest content with the idea that it does not matter what people think so long as they act with respect for others' rights. The purpose of Critical

Race Theory and diversity, equity and inclusion programmes is to help people understand the problem and work at improving not just practices but attitudes. So long as attitudes remain negative, the practices are at risk of not being implemented fully. A sincere effort to understand the feelings involved is crucial – for *feelings* lie at the root of the attitudes; and this means each person's own private feelings. As a start one can test them against the contents of Peggy McIntosh's knapsack, and *mutatis mutandis* for other arenas of discrimination and injustice, denial or exclusion.

For example: if a person is hostile to the idea of transwomen being treated as women, the questions he needs to ask himself are: is he harmed or threatened in any way by this? Are his assumptions about 'the way things should be' justified by anything other than what he is used to, or wishes to be the case, or by conventional attitudes themselves, a matter merely of conceptual familiarity or habit? What cost does he think he is going to bear personally if society is comfortable with there being transwomen, and what harm does he think society itself will suffer? Given that there are concerns in some quarters about women's spaces (using the phrase to include e.g. women's sports), does he think it beyond the competence or intelligence of society to find ways to accommodate all the interests involved?

An objection raised in this and other connections is 'self-identification'. There is scepticism about self-identification (as a woman or a man, as a person of colour, as a Native American, as an Aboriginal Australian). Can a person be a woman because she says she is? As Pretendian controversies illustrate, some identity groups reject the self-identification of aspirant members, the implication being that there have to be adequate grounds justifying the assignment. In the case of self-identification as a member of a racial or ethnic group, there are indeed objective grounds available in descent or genetic testing. In the gender case, by contrast, sceptics point to the apparent arbitrariness of self-identification, the grounds consisting wholly in individuals' self-understanding of who – of what – they are, with nothing external to the claim itself (so sceptics say) in support. This scepticism leads to the idea that malign men will claim to 'feel' that they are women in order to get into women's toilets and prisons for unpleasant purposes. But even supposing this happens, it is more than ungenerous and unkind not to take self-identificatory claims seriously, it is mistaken – for there are indeed objective grounds: in the cogency of the avowal, the consistency of the claim, the conformity of the claim to how it is lived out, and the claimant's preparedness to bear the costs of so identifying in a not very receptive society. If it is harder to live in the wrong gender than to bear the cost of living in the right one, the self-identification justifies itself.

Do people have a human right to self-identify as what they wish to be? They certainly have an interest that they are entitled to assert if it does not violate the rights of others. A straightforward interpretation of the rights to privacy, beliefs, expression, and entitlement to the respect due to human dignity, implies that such an interest could only legitimately be gainsaid if it violated someone else's rights. Whether it is itself an individual right might by analogy be retrofitted, so to say, from the idea of a 'right to national self-determination', discussed – sceptically – earlier. Since the scepticism about 'nations' turns on their being artificial (constructed) entities, and since gender and race are argued on persuasive grounds to be artificial constructs likewise, the analogy might be closer than one thinks; but if so, in light of the 'interests–rights' distinction, they all fall on the former side. But to say this is not one whit to gainsay their importance.

Independently of the ideal of changing attitudes, rooting out discriminatory practices and structures is a must. The question to be asked is a simple one: whether anyone's human rights are violated by the way society, or this or that structure within it, operates. If they are, the practice must end, the structure must change. It is much simpler to say this than to effect the requisite changes and pay the costs they incur, but to point to effort and money as reasons for not doing it is an extremely feeble, indeed unacceptable, resort. In the end, *all* the issues surrounding social justice are issues about individual rights, as the foregoing has been at pains to argue; and in all but the most exigent and limited circumstances such as war or pandemic, they are sacrosanct. Their being so is established by what they address: the unacceptability to rational emotion of their absence, as happens in the atrocities of wars, genocides, oppressions, and the injustices and even horrors of enacted prejudice and discrimination.

Respecting someone's right to an opinion, and the expression of it, which one finds abominable, is hard. Seeing such views put into practice and harming others is even harder. Combatting abominable views and harmful practices is a social duty. It is just as hard to accept that Aristotle's Principle must apply, because how one carries out that duty matters too. Amassing better evidence and employing stronger arguments, influencing the direction of public policy, keeping faith with education – these are the methods that some activists are understandably but mistakenly impatient with. But they offer a better chance of advancing the aims of creating a fair and inclusive society than by generating obduracies through hostility and the denial to others of what one wishes for oneself and those one cares about: a full application of human rights.[7]

One must never forget that those who combat discrimination once did not even have the right to demand their rights. Since the mid-twentieth century the Western world has been engaged in a transition, a major readjustment, away from millennia-long oppressions and towards justice, led by the discriminated-against themselves. Social and mainstream media emphasise extreme statements and actions in support of rights and (by their opponents) in defence of interests: this should not be allowed to distract from the important fact that underlying the noise is an historical struggle for equality of rights for every individual.

There is *convivencia* when everyone's rights are respected, for in their practical application there is social and economic justice, the end and aim of progressive endeavour. By concentrating explicitly and wholeheartedly on *rights*, there can be victory for all in the 'woke wars'. That is the road to *pax humana*.

NOTES

Preface

All website links were correct as of 25 September 2024.

1 There is something of a consensus, at least at time of writing, that what brought the long-standing issues to a head was the advent of social media platforms at the end of the first decade of the twenty-first century, together with the rightward trend of politics in 'advanced democracies' as well as elsewhere, and particular circumstances such as Covid-19 and its impact through lockdowns, disagreements over vaccinations and masking, interruptions to education and social activities, and economic effects. This version of a 'perfect storm' theory might have a considerable degree of truth, especially as regards social media, which enormously enables the spread of information, opinion and debate, but also misinformation and much intemperate expression which in turn create silos,

NOTES

divisions and hostilities. Though there is much of value in what social media enables, its negative aspects are beyond doubt and very widespread. However, the issues fundamentally at stake in the 'woke wars' long predate social media, and have to be addressed independently of what from time to time triggers a greater than usual outburst of activity around them.

Introduction

1 In *Towards the Light* (in the US *Towards the Light of Liberty*) (Bloomsbury, 2007), I recount the efforts made from the beginning of the modern era (the sixteenth century CE) towards the attainment of a general application of ideas of human rights and civil liberties – chief among them freedom of expression, the ending of slavery, workers' rights, equality of the sexes, the ending of discrimination against homosexuals and the extension of democratic participation. In *Liberty in the Age of Terror* (Bloomsbury, 2009), I discuss the way states responding to threats of terrorism voluntarily restricted civil liberties as a putative means of self-defence, arguing that this was to hand the victory to those who wished to reverse the gains of broadly Enlightenment values in the relevant respects.
2 Once individual rights are fully respected questions of capabilities will be potentiated or enabled: see Amartya Sen, *Commodities and Capabilities* (Oxford University Press, new ed. 1999), Martha Nussbaum *Creating Capabilities* (Harvard University Press, 2013).
3 The point about the appearance of conflicts of rights was well made by Craig Stanbury in personal communication.

4 Ethics is not the same thing as morals; the word 'ethics' derives from Greek *ethos* meaning 'character', and concerns how we live and the values we live by. 'Morals' comes from an adaptation by Cicero of Latin *mores*, meaning 'convention' or 'practice' to denote the duties and obligations people have to one another. Ethical considerations sometimes conflict with the moral outlook of a given society – for example, in Western countries within living memory the attitude that homosexuality is immoral was challenged by ethical considerations about what society's attitudes should be in relation to homosexuals – and the ethical considerations won.

5 These are facts. In 1997 I ran a conference on the question of the universality of human rights in Hong Kong in the hope of fortifying, by airing, their significance in light of the return that year of the colony to the People's Republic of China. Representatives from mainland China were adamant that the exigencies of building the country's future required individuals to submit not merely their personal interests but their rights to the cause of the greater good. In 1990 the Cairo Declaration on Human Rights in Islam was adopted by the Organisation of Islamic Cooperation (OIC), stating throughout that its principles are subject to Shariah law and can only be interpreted in the light of the latter. This law, in turn, denies a number of significant rights claimed by the UN Declaration.

1 Divide and Cancel

1 The first uses of the phrase in the 1970s were an ironic reminder of the concept's employment in Nazi Germany and Soviet Russia

NOTES

where it denoted the idea of required political orthodoxy, aka obedience to the Party.

2 See Miranda Fricker, 'Silence and Institutional Prejudice', in Sharon Crasnow and Anita Superson (eds) *Out from the Shadows: Analytical Feminist Contributions to Traditional Philosophy* (Oxford University Press, 2012).

3 The horror of the act consists in its being an indiscriminate murder of many non-combatants – civilians – in a treacherous, unexpected attack. Even if the indiscriminate murder of civilians is advertised as likely to happen, and is expected by the civilian population who have therefore made preparations to defend and protect themselves, e.g. as in circumstances of declared international war, the indiscriminate nature of the attack and its target make it a crime by the 1977 First Protocol to the Fourth Geneva Convention. I discuss this in my *Among the Dead Cities* (Walker Books, 2006). My drawing a comparison in that book between the indiscriminate bombing of civilian populations by the UK and the US in the Second World War and the 9/11 attack occasioned the only disagreement ever to occur between myself and my late friend Christopher Hitchens. To this day the US has not ratified the 1977 First Protocol.

4 The burial at sea was conducted according to Islamic rites.

5 The 'Melian Dialogue' is instructive; a good short summary is provided at: www.nku.edu/~weirk/ir/melian.html. Interestingly, the Melian representatives at the parley requested that it be private, because they feared that the eloquence of the Athenians would sway the population in favour of submission. The case for democratic procedures could make something of this.

6 I give a fuller of account of the Boyle Thomas incident in A.C. Grayling, *The Frontiers of Knowledge* (Viking, 2021), pp. 200–2.
7 An excellent discussion relevant to this book is Martha Nussbaum, *Anger and Forgiveness* (Oxford University Press 2016).
8 Two examples that can serve for many are a video made by the 'Good Liars' team of interviews with Trump supporters waiting in line for a rally at Greensboro, North Carolina: 'Pranksters Ask Trump Rally-Goers Some Simple Questions', Yahoo News, 18 April 2024: www.yahoo.com/news/pranksters-ask-trump-rally-goers-082058489.html, and a BBC documentary on the 'Christian Nationalist' Right: 'How a New Christian Right Is Changing US Politics', 22 November 2022.
9 This is not to claim insight I could not have as a white person. See Glenn C. Loury, *The Anatomy of Racial Inequality* (new ed.) (Harvard University Press, 2021); Ijeoma Oluo, *So You Want to Talk about Race* (Seal Press, 2018); Tanya Maria Golash-Boza, *Race and Racisms* (Oxford University Press, 2021); Joe R. Feagin, *Racist America* (4th ed.) (Routledge, 2018); Reni Eddo-Lodge, *Why I'm No Longer Talking To White People about Race* (Bloomsbury, 2017); Ibram X. Kendi, *Stamped from the Beginning* (Bold Type Books, 2018).
10 See Miranda Fricker, 'Fault and No-Fault Responsibility for Implicit Prejudice – A Space for Epistemic "Agent-Regret"', in Michael Brady and Miranda Fricker (eds), *The Epistemic Life of Groups* (Oxford University Press, 2016) for insights important not just for this point but for the argument in what follows.
11 Cardinal Richelieu once remarked that he could use two lines from anything anyone wrote to hang him. He meant that by clever insinuation and manipulation he could prove anyone guilty of

something. Often a superficial, partial or deliberately distorted reading of something someone did or said can be given the Richelieu treatment. Indeed this happens all the time; it is a stock-in-trade of political quarrels, and has become likewise in the so-called woke wars. No one is safe from the Richelieu treatment if someone is determined to find a cause for complaint. And the principle *audi alteram partem* is observed more in the breach than ever.

2 Ideas and Orientations

1 Almost every translation of Genesis 3:6 has Eve desiring 'wisdom', but the *Message Bible* says, 'When the Woman saw that the tree looked like good eating and realized what she would get out of it – she'd know everything! – she took and ate the fruit.'
2 In *Philosophy and Life* (Penguin, 2023) I discuss the different views of Soren Kierkegaard and Immanuel Kant about the Abraham–Isaac story, siding with the latter. *Mutatis mutandis* all of Jahweh's more sanguinary urgings admit of the Kantian treatment.
3 See, for a helpful brief survey, Society for Old Testament Study, 'Law in the Old Testament': www.sots.ac.uk/wiki/law-in-the-old-testament/.
4 Gary A. Anderson, *Sin: A History* (Yale University Press, 2009).
5 The category of mortal sin includes 'neglect of Sunday obligation', a practical addition presumably, since this is when the collection plate (offering plate) is passed round; in some parishes, twice in the same Mass. Apparently this practice has diminished since Covid, presumably for prudential reasons at first.

6   David M. Knight, 'The Difference between Sin and Crime', *La Croix International*, 16 April 2024: https://international.la-croix.com/news/ethics/the-difference-between-sin-and-crime/12859#.

7   See e.g. Kate Samuelson, 'The Countries Where Men and Women Can Be Stoned to Death', *The Week*, 14 July 2022: https://theweek.com/news/crime/957354/the-countries-where-men-women-can-be-stoned-to-death. Countries where death is a legal punishment for adultery include Saudi Arabia, Sudan, Iran, Somalia, Yemen, Afghanistan and some Muslim-majority states in Nigeria. Adultery is still a crime in two US states; it is a felony in Oklahoma and a Class 3 misdemeanour in Arizona; at time of writing it was in the process of being decriminalised in New York State.

8   *Report of the Committee on Homosexual Offences and Prostitution*, Command 247 (1956–7), full text available at: https://archive.org/details/the-wolfenden-report-report-of-the-committee-on-homosexual-offenses-and-prostitution-image-large.

9   Patrick, Lord Devlin, *The Enforcement of Morals* (Oxford University Press, 1959).

10 Criminal Law Amendment Act 1885. Anal sex (sodomy, buggery), whether homosexual or heterosexual, was outlawed by the Buggery Act 1533, the penalty being hanging; the last two people hanged for sodomy were James Pratt and John Smith in 1835. The death penalty for sodomy was rescinded in 1861, but the Indian Penal Code of 1860 criminalised homosexuality, and served as a basis for similar laws elsewhere in the British Empire; they or their derivatives still exist in thirty-four member states of the Commonwealth. Oscar Wilde was convicted under the 1885 Act, which brought all forms of male homosexual behaviour under

NOTES

legal proscription, not just sodomy, even if private; letters between gay lovers were enough for conviction. Anal sex ceased to be illegal in England and Wales in 1994 (Criminal Justice and Public Order Act 1994 §143). Lesbianism has never been proscribed by law. Prosecutions of trans men married to women (trans men *in sensu* women presenting or self-identifying as men in order to enter marriage with a woman) were based on indictments of fraud, because before the Married Women's Property Act 1882 a wife's property became her husband's on marriage.

11 Not just 'unnatural' sexual behaviour but unlicensed heterosexually 'normal' behaviour was biblically proscribed: 'Suppose a man meets a young woman, a virgin who is engaged to be married, and he has sexual intercourse with her. If this happens within a town, you must take both of them to the gates of that town and stone them to death' (Deut. 22:23–4).

12 H.L.A. Hart, *The Concept of Law* (Oxford University Press, 1961).

13 John Stuart Mill, *On Liberty* (1859). Available on Gutenberg at: www.gutenberg.org/files/34901/34901-h/34901-h.htm.

14 See 'Abortion, *Roe v Wade*, and Pre-Dobbs Doctrine', *Constitution Annotated* on Fourteenth Amendment: https://constitution.congress.gov/browse/essay/amdt14-S1-6-4-1/ALDE_00013276/.

15 *Dobbs v Jackson Women's Health Organization*, No. 19–1392, 597 U.S. 215 (2022): www.supremecourt.gov/opinions/21pdf/19-1392_6j37.pdf.

16 *Roe v Wade*, 410 U.S. 113 (1973): https://supreme.justia.com/cases/federal/us/410/113/#:~:text=A%20person%20may%20choose%20to,and%2028%20weeks%20after%20conception. As was pointed out in the 2022 decision, appeal to the right to privacy

rested not just on the Fourteenth Amendment, but also on the First, Fourth, Fifth and Ninth Amendments.

17 In my *Philosophy and Life* I advert to an important point: 'It might come as a surprise to some to see that ethics and morals, although of course intimately connected, are distinguishable ... Ethics is a more inclusive matter than morality; it concerns character whereas morality concerns actions. Our actions will mainly of course flow from our character, but the targets of enquiry in ethics (seeking answers to "What sort of person shall I be?") and in debates about morality ("What is the right thing to do in this case?") are obviously not the same'.

18 For reasons of economy the fact that the Supreme Court in *Dobbs* returned the question of abortion to the states is not discussed; the effect of denying abortion as a right under the *federal* constitution is the crucial point.

19 For an extensive overview see Catherine Nixey, *Heresy* (Picador, 2024).

20 An illustrative selection of studies of punishment: Bruce N. Waller, Elizabeth Shaw and Farah Focquaert (eds), *The Routledge Handbook of the Philosophy and Science of Punishment* (Routledge, 2020); David Boonin, *The Problem of Punishment* (Cambridge University Press, 2008); Michel Foucault, *Discipline and Punish* (Vintage, 1995); Michael Tonry, *Why Punish? How Much?* (Oxford University Press, 2010); Matthew C. Altman, *A Theory of Legal Punishment* (Routledge, 2021); Alan Brudner, *Punishment and Freedom* (Oxford University Press, 2009); Michael Davis, *To Make the Punishment Fit the Crime* (Westview Press, 1992); Deirdre Golash, *The Case against Punishment* (New York University Press, 2005); Matt Matravers, *Justice and Punishment* (Oxford University

NOTES

Press, 2000); Martha Nussbaum, *Anger and Forgiveness* (Oxford University Press, 2016); George Sher, *Desert* (Princeton University Press, 1987); C.L. Ten, *Crime, Guilt and Punishment* (Oxford University Press, 1987); Michael J. Zimmerman, *The Immorality of Punishment* (Broadview Press, 2011).

21 I discuss an instance of this in an appendix to *Philosophy and Life* as an illustration of different Stoic views about legal sanctions.

22 Golash, *Case against Punishment*.

23 Nghiem L. Nguyen, 'Roman Rape', *Michigan Journal of Gender and Law*, Vol. 13, No. 1, 2006.

24 On 'chattel' status or its analogues, *vide* Kevin C. Paul, 'Private/Property', *Minnesota Journal of Law and Inequality*, Vol. 7, No. 3, 1989.

25 *Vide* Golash, *Case against Punishment*.

26 Solitary confinement is likely to achieve some of the principal aims of punishment in a much shorter time than imprisonment in its more usual forms. It is a psychologically harsher treatment, however, which might be regarded by some as the reason for its greater efficacy. Within prison regimes its deterrent effect on disruptive behaviour is notably successful. In moral criticism of penology it is regarded as cruel, a form of mental torture.

27 I point out in my *Among the Dead Cities* that both US military and civilian attitudes to the Japanese, not least because of the latter's treatment of US prisoners of war, underlay the temporising of moral considerations in the turn to the bombing strategy of XXI Bomber Command in the Pacific theatre. In Europe, US bombing was theoretically restricted to economic and military targets, undertaken in daylight, unlike the RAF Bomber Command's 'carpet bombing' of cities and their populations by night, but in the Pacific theatre under General Curtis LeMay carpet bombing

('strategic' bombing) was adopted, culminating in the eventual use of two atom bombs.

28 President Trump added determination to erect a wall along the US's southern border 'to keep out criminals and rapists' to efforts to ban Muslim immigrants.

29 A very good survey is provided by John A. Powell and Stephen Menendian in 'The Problem of Othering', *Othering and Belonging* (2024): www.otheringandbelonging.org/the-problem-of-othering/.

30 I deal with these points in detail in *The Good State* (Oneworld, 2020).

31 The Soviet Union, its Eastern European satellite states, the People's Republic of China in their command-economy heyday, and North Korea still, provide examples of states where economic control almost immediately required draconian control of the population itself.

32 Michel Foucault *vide* e.g. *Madness and Civilization, The Birth of the Clinic, Discipline and Punish.*

33 Derrida *vide* e.g. *Writing and Difference.*

34 Peggy McIntosh, 'White Privilege: Unpacking the Invisible Knapsack', *Peace and Freedom Magazine*, July/August 1989.

35 One of very many examples of Pretendians or alleged Pretendians is the actor Johnny Depp claiming Cherokee descent when he played Tonto in *The Lone Ranger* (Disney, 2013). Other cases include Andrea Smith of the University of California, and Kay LeClaire, an artist based in Wisconsin, who were challenged over claims to be Native American; Jessica Krug of George Washington University and Rachel Dolezal of the Spokane chapter of the National Association for the Advancement of Colored People who claimed to be Black; while Berkeley professor Elizabeth

Hoover, whose family had long led her to believe she was Native American, concluded after research on her family history that she was white. See S. Jaschik, 'Berkeley Professor Admits that She's White', *Inside Higher Ed*, 8 May 2023: www.insidehighered.com/news/faculty-issues/diversity-equity/2023/05/08/berkeley-professor-admits-shes-white.

36 To avoid the grammatical clumsiness and sometimes ambiguity of 'they' as a universal non-gendered pronoun I alternate uses of 'he' and 'she' as equitably as possible, at times by context.

37 'How Bill Maher Defines "Woke"', *CNN*, 2 March 2023: www.youtube.com/watch?v=tzwC-10O0cw.

38 Pew Research Center, 'Americans and "Cancel Culture"' (2021): www.pewresearch.org/internet/2021/05/19/americans-and-cancel-culture-where-some-see-calls-for-accountability-others-see-censorship-punishment/.

39 I do not include 'religion' for reasons explained later.

40 The best discussion of this – of the uses and considerations of 'cancelling' as a strategy for campaigners – is Adrienne Maree Brown's *We Will Not Cancel Us* (AK Press, 2021).

41 'Flood the zone with shit': in Tim Lister, 'How Europe's Populists Are Following the Steve Bannon Playbook', *CNN*, 23 June 2018: https://edition.cnn.com/2018/06/23/europe/salvini-bannon-lister-intl/index.html.

3 Othering, Excluding and Cancelling *Groups*

1 Edward Peters, *Inquisition* (University of California Press, 1989) is the chief locus of revisionary study of the 'myth of the

Inquisition'. Peters argues that the 'Black Inquisition' portrait given by anti-Catholic and anti-clericalism writers after the Reformation began to be examined more judiciously by Henry Charles Lea at the end of the nineteenth century.
2 William Monter, *Frontiers of Heresy: The Spanish Inquisition from the Basque Lands to Sicily* (Cambridge University Press, 2003).
3 Joseph Blötzer, 'Inquisition', in *The Catholic Encyclopedia*, Vol. 8 (Robert Appleton Company, 1910), available at *New Advent*: www.newadvent.org/cathen/08026a.htm.
4 Peters, *Inquisition*.
5 W.A. Sibly and M.D. Sibly, *The Chronicle of William of Puylaurens: The Albigensian Crusade and Its Aftermath* (Boydell Press, 2003); Zoe Oldenbourg, *Massacre at Montsegur: A History of the Albigensian Crusade* (Phoenix, 2000).
6 Blötzer, 'Inquisition'.
7 Malcolm Barber, *The Cathars: Dualist Heretics in Languedoc in the High Middle Ages* (Longman, 2000).
8 Peter of Les Vaux-de-Cernay, Historia Albigensis, translated by W.A. Sibly and M.D. Sibly (Boydell Press, 1988).
9 Thomas Aquinas, *Summa Theologica,* Part II, 1 *quaestiones,* 85–9. In preference to the 61-volume Blackfriars edition one might consult the translation by Timothy McDermott, *Summa Theologiae: A Concise Translation* (Eyre and Spottiswoode, 1989).
10 Grayling, *Towards the Light*.
11 I put scare quotes around the word 'race' because, for reasons later given, I am sceptical that the word has any more than a meaning socially constructed on morally irrelevant factors such as skin colour and other physical features.

NOTES

12 Hans Medick, translated by Pamela Selwyn, 'Historical Event and Contemporary Experience: The Capture and Destruction of Magdeburg in 1631', *History Workshop Journal*, Vol. 52, No. 1, 2001.
13 A.C. Grayling, *War: An Inquiry* (Yale University Press, 2017).
14 Grayling, *Among the Dead Cities*.
15 Ibid.
16 *Vide* Norman M. Naimark, *Stalin's Genocides* (Princeton University Press, 2010); Robert Conquest, *The Harvest of Sorrow* (Oxford University Press, 1987).
17 Lebin Yan, 'I Participated in the Cultural Revolution Activities in Guangxi', *Yanhuang Chunqiu*, quoted in *Social Science History*, Vol. 46, No. 1, Spring 2022: https://doi.org/10.1017/ssh.2021.42. I had first-hand testimony from former Red Guards while living in China in the early 1980s, with one of whom, Xu You Yu, I later co-authored a book on the history of the Chinese Communist Party, *The Long March to the Fourth of June*, under the joint pseudonym of 'Li Xiao Jun', putatively translated by 'E.J. Griffiths' (my grandmother's name) (Duckworth, 1989). The pseudonym would be recognisable as such to a Chinese reader; it could be translated as 'Little General Jones'.
18 Martin Singer, 'Educated Youth and the Cultural Revolution in China', *Michigan Papers in Chinese Studies*, No. 10 (1971).
19 Ibid., p. 5.
20 Mao Zedong, 'On Practice: On the Relation Between Knowledge and Practice, Between Knowing and Doing', in *Selected Works of Mao Zedong*, Vol. I (Foreign Language Press, 1965), p. 299.
21 Singer, 'Educated Youth'.
22 Ibid.

DISCRIMINATIONS

23 Chinese Communist Party documents cited in ibid., pp. 33–4.
24 Ibid., p. 52.
25 Klaus Mehnert, *Peking and the New Left* (University of California Press, 1969), p. 93.
26 Singer, 'Educated Youth', p. 38.
27 It was while living in China – in Beijing, teaching at the Chinese Academy of Social Sciences, some of whose members had been Red Guards and others victimised by them during the Cultural Revolution's height in 1966–8 (the revolution itself lasted until the downfall of the Gang of Four in 1976) – that I came to appreciate how vivid and painful memories of the Cultural Revolution were; some of the accounts – usually whispered, even in the relative security of a park or large restaurant – of what colleagues and friends experienced was harrowing.
28 Surinder S. Jodhka, *Caste in Contemporary India* (2nd ed.) (Routledge, 2017). *Vide* also Susan Bayley, 'Caste, Society and Politics in India from the 18th Century to the Modern Age', in *The New Cambridge History of India*, Vol. 4 (Cambridge University Press, 1999).
29 Bayley, 'Caste', note 57.
30 Jodhka, *Caste*, Introduction.
31 Ibid.

4 Othering, Excluding and Cancelling *Individuals*

1 Richard Ellmann, *Oscar Wilde* (Vintage, 1988).
2 I tell the story of Michael Servetus and the consequences of his persecution by Calvin in more detail in *Towards the Light*, there

NOTES

exploring how his execution sparked a backlash, much aided by Sebastian Castellio's eloquent advocacy on the matter, against any Protestant denomination mimicking the harsher aspects of the Inquisition in enforcing orthodoxy.

3 Calvin, *Institutes of the Christian Religion*: www.ccel.org/ccel/calvin/institutes.toc.html.

4 Grayling, *Towards the Light*.

5 Peter Brown, *The Body and Society* (Columbia University Press, 1988).

6 The article, and its footnoted references, at: https://en.wikipedia.org/wiki/Sexual_coercion_among_animals#:~:text=Males%20of%20many%20species%20simply,and%20easily%20accessible%20to%20males, is a salutary introduction to this topic.

7 'Rapist' and 'Lothario/sex pest' ('sex pest' denoting catcallers, flashers, over-persistent attempts at chatting up) are intended to mark the opposite ends of a spectrum, between which more serious forms of harassment such as grabbing, stalking and revenge porn figure. As Hannah Haseloff remarked to me, 'The latter are short of rape but still dangerous, threatening and potentially illegal. A lot of those offenders escalate (Sarah Everard's murderer comes to mind). Some of them need punishment, not education ... perhaps the anger on social media might reflect a lack of real-world consequences for sexual offenders (conviction rate c.1%)'. See 'Why Do So Few Rape Cases Go to Court?', *BBC News*, 27 May 2022: www.bbc.co.uk/news/uk-48095118.

8 Accounts of Victorian medical interventions to stop people – not least children – from masturbating are horror stories. See

Diane Mason, *The Secret Vice* (Manchester University Press, 2013).

9 Todd Spangler, '"Dilbert" Comic Strip Dropped by Newspapers over Scott Adams' Racist Comments', *Variety*, 25 February 2023: https://variety.com/2023/digital/news/dilbert-canceled-newspapers-scott-adams-racist-1235535643/.

10 Lisette Voytko-Best, 'Billionaire No More: Kanye West's Antisemitism Obliterates His Net Worth as Adidas Cuts Ties', *Forbes*, 25 October 2022: www.forbes.com/sites/lisettevoytko/2022/10/25/billionaire-no-more-kanye-wests-anti-semitism-obliterates-his-net-worth-as-adidas-cuts-ties/?sh=1c1ef5f517e7.

5 Right(s) and Wrong(s)

1 Amartya Sen, *Identity and Violence: The Illusion of Destiny* (Penguin Books, 2008).

2 At time of writing Israel has a population of 9.5 million, of whom two million are Israeli Arabs.

3 Megan Gannon and LiveScience, 'Race is a Social Construct, Scientists Argue', *Scientific American*, 5 February 2016: www.scientificamerican.com/article/race-is-a-social-construct-scientists-argue/.

4 National Institutes of Health Office of Research on Women's Health, 'Office of Management and Budget (OMB) Standards', *NIH Inclusion Outreach Toolkit: How to Engage, Recruit, and Retain Women in Clinical Research*: https://orwh.od.nih.gov/toolkit/other-relevant-federal-policies/OMB-standards.

NOTES

5 In June 2023 the Supreme Court decision in *Students for Fair Admissions Inc. v President and Fellows of Harvard University* brought affirmative action to an end after forty years. See: www.washingtonpost.com/documents/4ff078d7-f01b-4533-8edc-5a894fc82cde.pdf?itid=lk_inline_manual_3. Ironically, the majority cited the Fourteenth Amendment's Equal Protection Clause as a key to deciding whether affirmative action is constitutional; this is the clause cited by the justices in *Roe v Wade* regarding abortion. Thus the Trump court reversed two progressive measures on the same principle.

6 See this Quora post, for instance: https://africa.quora.com/https-www-quora-com-Are-Ethiopians-half-white-Why-do-they-look-different-than-other-Africans-answer-Jason-Ford-104.

7 The right to remain silent without prejudice was removed ('modified' say neutral accounts of the matter) from UK citizens (technically, subjects of the Crown rather than citizens) – having previously been removed from terrorist suspects and those accused of serious fraud – by the Conservative government's Criminal Justice and Public Order Act of 1994. I took part in the campaign against the change, and presented to and discussed with Tony Blair, then Shadow Home Secretary, arguments for him to use in his challenge to this aspect of the Bill in the House of Commons. The subsequent Labour administration with Blair as Prime Minister did not reverse the change.

8 Jeremy Bentham, *Anarchical Fallacies* (1796).

9 See the Capuchin monkey fairness experiment and Frans de Waal's comments on the phenomenon in other species: 'Two Monkeys Were Paid Unequally: Excerpt from Frans de Waal's

TED Talk', TED Blog Video, 4 April 2013: www.youtube.com/watch?v=meiU6TxysCg.

10 See David Graeber and David Wengrow, *The Dawn of Everything* (Allen Lane, 2021), which has interesting things to say about early human societies and the emergence of inequality, taking Rousseau as an inspiration.

11 I made a number of *amicus curiae* submissions to the courts in support of petitioners in such cases, arguing this precise point beginning with the Diane Petty case in 2001. See A.C. Grayling 'The Right to Die', *British Medical Journal*, Vol. 330, 2005: https://doi.org/10.1136/bmj.330.7495.799.

12 Some think that ideas of 'nationhood' long predate this – think of the 'Nations' into which students of the University of Paris were grouped in medieval times. In fact the term implied geography and language, not citizenship; the modern sense of 'nation' involves this latter equally modern concept as well as the idea of ethnic belonging. Russian irredentism in respect of Russian-speaking majorities in east European countries is predicated on this blur of ideas.

13 James Mayall, 'International Society, State Sovereignty, and National Self-Determination', in John Breuilly (ed.), *The Oxford Handbook of the History of Nationalism* (Oxford University Press, 2013).

14 I was among them; see A.C. Grayling, *Against All Gods* (Bloomsbury, 2007), *To Set Prometheus Free* (Oberon Books, 2012), *The God Argument* (Bloomsbury, 2013) and variously in the essay collection *The Meaning of Things* and its successors. Richard Dawkins, *The God Delusion* (Bantam, 2006); Christopher

NOTES

Hitchens, *God Is Not Great* (Twelve Books, 2007); Daniel Dennett, *Breaking the Spell* (Viking, 2006); and Sam Harris, *The End of Faith* (W.W. Norton, 2004) were grouped as 'the Four Horsemen of New Atheism'. There is nothing new about atheism.

15 For surveys see Peter Hunt, 'Slavery', in *The Cambridge World History: Volume 4: A World with States, Empires and Networks 1200 BCE–900 CE* (Cambridge University Press, 2015); Susanne Everett, *The History of Slavery* (Grange Books, 1997); T.C. Holt's otherwise excellent *Children of Fire* (New York: Hill and Wang, 2011) omits from the history of enslavement of Africans the Arab involvement, which was even longer, more numerous and no less hideous than the Atlantic trade.

16 It is estimated that 90% of slaves taken in the Atlantic trade were captured by other Africans; see Linda M. Heywood, 'Slavery and Its Transformation in the Kingdom of Kongo', *Journal of African History*, Vol. 50, 2009.

17 There are many accounts; examples occur in *The Last Journals of David Livingstone in Central Africa* (Cambridge University Press, 1875).

18 This registers a change of mind on my part regarding one aspect of the reparations issue, viz. the value of formal apologies by descendants of those who profited from the trade, including implicated states themselves. In chairing a debate at the British Empire and Commonwealth Museum in Bristol in 2006 about whether the city should apologise for its involvement in the slave trade, I iterated a point I made in an article in the *Independent* the preceding day ('Apologising for the Slave Trade

Would Be a Futile Gesture', *Independent*, 11 May 2006: www.independent.co.uk/voices/commentators/a-c-grayling-apologising-for-the-slave-trade-would-be-a-futile-gesture-6101161.html) to that effect, arguing that the best way to address the history of slavery was to end present-day slavery. See also my article for *Prospect*: 'Grayling's Question: Can the Past Entitle Us to Apologies, Reparations or Recognition Today?', *Prospect*, 11 December 2008: www.prospectmagazine.co.uk/culture/58628/graylings-question-can-the-past-entitle-us-to-apologies-reparations-or-recognition-today. As the main text here indicates, though I continue to think that addressing slavery in today's world is without question an essential endeavour, forms of reparation for the current legacy of past slavery should also be implemented.

19 In founding the TransAfrica organisation African American lawyer and activist Randall Robinson argued that the losses sustained by African Americans from slavery, racism and their lingering impact amount to $1.4 trillion. Other estimates put the total closer to $5 trillion. On this latter calculation a sum of $200,000 is owed to each African American alive at the time the calculation was made, which was the year 1999. See Randall Robinson, 'He Drove the First US Stake in South African Apartheid', *Journal of Blacks in Higher Education*, Vol. 24, 1999; and 'Six White Congressmen Endorse Reparations for Slavery', *Journal of Blacks in Higher Education*, Vol. 27, 2000.

20 The Heirs of Slavery organisation, of people who benefit from their ancestors' activities as slave-owners or slavers, is an admirable instance of personal recognition and activism in reparation: www.heirsofslavery.org.

NOTES

21 'Council to Debate Reparations and Bristol's Involvement in Afrikan Enslavement', Bristol Green Party, 2 March 2021: https://bristolgreenparty.org.uk/council-to-debate-reparations-and-bristols-involvement-in-afrikan-enslavement/.
22 CARICOM, 'Ten Point Plan for Reparatory Justice': https://caricom.org/caricom-ten-point-plan-for-reparatory-justice/.
23 International Labour Organization, 'Global Estimates of Modern Slavery' (2022): www.ilo.org/publications/major-publications/global-estimates-modern-slavery-forced-labour-and-forced-marriage.
24 As this book was coming to completion an article appeared in the *New York Times* calling for abolition of slavery in today's US prison system: Andrew Ross, Tommaso Bardelli and Aiyuba Thomas, 'End Legal Slavery in the United States', *New York Times*, 19 June 2024: www.nytimes.com/2024/06/19/opinion/juneteenth-slavery-prison.html?campaign_id=39&emc=edit_ty_20240622&instance_id=126892&nl=opinion-today&regi_id=4725588&segment_id=170266&te=1&user_id=8e449fee43aaeeef29cc4d8a189a0225.
25 Jonathan Haidt, *The Anxious Generation* (Allen Lane, 2024).

6 Concerns and Comparisons

1 Sabra L. Katz-Wise, 'Sexual Fluidity and the Diversity of Sexual Orientation', *Harvard Health Publishing*, 31 March 2022: www.health.harvard.edu/blog/sexual-fluidity-and-the-diversity-of-sexual-orientation-202203312717.

2 Madeline B. Deutsch, 'Overview of Gender-Affirming Treatments and Procedures', *UCSF Transgender Care & Treatment Guidelines*, 17 June 2016: https://transcare.ucsf.edu/guidelines/overview.

3 A selection of the literature on transgender issues should include Judith Butler, *Gender Trouble* (Routledge, 2006) and *Who's Afraid of Gender?* (Farrar, Straus and Giroux, 2024); Jamison Green, *Becoming a Visible Man* (2nd ed.) (Vanderbilt University Press, 2020); Diane Ehrensaft, *Gender Born, Gender Made* (rev. ed.) (The Experiment Publishing, 2011); Kate Bornstein, *Gender Outlaw* (2nd ed.) (Vintage, 2016); Stuart Biegel, *The Right to be Out* (2nd ed.) (University of Minnesota Press, 2018). See also Peggy Gillespie, *Authentic Selves* (Skinner House, 2023).

4 Katherine Schaeffer, 'For Women's History Month, a Look at Gender Gains – and Gaps – in the US', *Pew Research Center*, 27 February 2024: www.pewresearch.org/short-reads/2024/02/27/for-womens-history-month-a-look-at-gender-gains-and-gaps-in-the-us/.

5 Not all mothers were as patriotically enthusiastic about sending their sons to war as the 'Little Mother' whose letter to the *Morning Post* in 1916 became a celebrated part of First World War recruitment efforts in Britain; quoted disparagingly in Robert Graves' *Goodbye To All That* (1929), it is discussed along with less sanguine because less sanguinary attitudes at the 'Behind Their Lines' blogspot at: https://behindtheirlines.blogspot.com/2017/11/mothers-of-war.html. The 'Little Mother' reprised the Spartan mothers' adjuration to their sons, handing them their shields: 'Come back either with it or on it'.

NOTES

6 Jesse J. Holland, 'Report: How Black America Has Changed in 40 Years', *PBS News*, 17 May 2016: www.pbs.org/newshour/nation/report-black-america-doing-much-better-than-40-years-ago.

7 Abigail Thernstrom and Stephan Thernstrom, 'Black Progress: How Far We've Come, and How Far We Have to Go', *Brookings*, 1 March 1998: www.brookings.edu/articles/black-progress-how-far-weve-come-and-how-far-we-have-to-go/.

8 Janelle Jones, John Schmitt and Valerie Wilson, '50 Years after the Kerner Commission', *Economic Policy Institute*, 26 February 2018: www.epi.org/publication/50-years-after-the-kerner-commission/.

9 Ibid.

10 Ibid.

11 Sharon D. Wright Austin, 'Black Americans Mostly Left Behind by Progress since Dr King's Death', *Conversation*, 7 February 2018: https://theconversation.com/black-americans-mostly-left-behind-by-progress-since-dr-kings-death-89956. The references in her commentary are e.g. Ta-Nehisi Coates, *Between the World and Me* (Spiegal and Grau, 2015); Michelle Alexander, *The New Jim Crow* (New Press, 2010); Ben Carson (with Candy Carson), *One Nation: What We Can All Do to Save America's Future* (Sentinel, 2014); Thomas Sowell, *Discrimination and Disparities* (Basic Books, 2018).

12 Wright Austin, 'Black Americans'.

13 Nesrine Malik, 'How 50 Years of Racial Progress Fuelled a Global Movement against Racism', *Correspondent*, 9 July 2020: https://thecorrespondent.com/576/how-50-years-of-racial-progress-fuelled-a-global-movement-against-racism.

14 Christopher Rufo, 'The Courage of Our Convictions', *City Journal*, 21 April 2022: www.city-journal.org/article/the-courage-of-our-convictions.

15 Christopher Rufo, *America's Cultural Revolution* (Broadside Books, 2023); see David Volodzko, 'Book Review: Mein Kampf', *The Radicalist*, August 2023: www.theradicalist.com/p/book-review-mein-kampf, in which he argues that 'Marxist liberals use deceptive motte-and-bailey arguments to move the Overton window [the 'window of discourse'] ... I said this chapter [of *Mein Kampf*] can help us identify fascist trends in modern political movements. With that in mind, consider Hitler's points of contention and tell me if they sound familiar. He lists the mainstream liberal media, proselytizing liberal art – which today would be woke movies, Marxism, politically correct language, ethnic groups that do not assimilate to the nation's traditional culture, disrespect for authority such as police, anti-capitalist protests and disrespect for controversial historical figures'. See also Volodzko's YouTube vlog, 'How Marxism Subverted America': www.youtube.com/watch?v=qgcWV_ptS6s.

16 Richard F. Hamilton and Lowell L. Hargens, 'The Politics of the Professors', *Social Forces*, Vol. 71, 1993.

17 Ibid.

18 A cynic today might regard the large swing to business and technical subjects, serving the employability agenda in universities, and the attrition of the humanities, as a conspiracy to distract from socio-political debates so that the status quo is protected from scrutiny. Acknowledging that in a highly technologised and economically-integrated world, business and STEM are at a premium, as is employability in the highly competitive situation this creates, one is nevertheless reminded of what Nobel laureate physicist Steven Weinberg said of President Ronald Reagan's 'Star

Wars' initiative (paraphrasing): 'It doesn't worry me that the President doesn't know science, but it does worry me that he doesn't know history and philosophy, because if he did he would not dream of doing this'.

19 Peter Warren, 'Delta Force', *Heritage Foundation Policy Review*, 1994. For comparison, the latest study available at time of writing (2024) found that between 9 and 13% of university faculty were 'strongly conservative': Alex Walters, 'Actually, There Are More Conservatives on the Faculty Than You Think, Study Finds', *Chronicle of Higher Education*, 26 July 2024: www.chronicle.com/article/actually-there-are-more-conservatives-on-the-faculty-than-you-think-study-finds?utm_source=Iterable&utm_medium=email&utm_campaign=campaign_10586484_nl_Academe-Today_date_20240729&sra=true.

20 Moira Weigl, 'Political Correctness: How the Right Invented a Phantom Enemy', *Guardian*, 30 November 2016.

21 Ibid.

22 Richard Bernstein, 'A "Minute of Hatred" in Chapel Hill', *New York Times*, 25 September 1998, reprinted in Robert L. Stone (ed.), *Essays on The Closing of the American Mind* (Chicago Review Press, 1989).

23 Weigl, 'Political Correctness'.

24 Ibid.

25 Dinesh D'Souza, *Illiberal Education: The Politics of Race and Sex on Campus* (Vintage, 1992).

26 John K. Wilson, *The Myth of Political Correctness* (Duke University Press, 1995).

27 'Excerpts from President's Speech to University of Michigan Graduates', *New York Times*, 5 May 1991.

28 Ibid.
29 To declare a position, I am an admirer of these organisations, and of the courageous individual stand of Greta Thunberg. See my previous book, *For the Good of the World* (Oneworld, 2022).
30 See Florida Governor Ron DeSantis's initiative on universities in his state: Matthew Arrojas and Chloe Appleby, 'DeSantis' Plan to Reconstruct Higher Education in Florida Explained', *BestColleges*, 7 August 2023: www.bestcolleges.com/news/analysis/desantis-plan-to-reconstruct-higher-education-in-florida/.
31 Rufo, 'Courage of Our Convictions'.

7 The Bottom Line

1 Those who do not understand the motives of some 'woke warriors' would do well to look at accounts of the experience of individuals who have been on the front line of painful victimhood. For one of many examples, read Robert Samuels, 'Public Memories. Private Struggles', *Washington Post*, 22 June 2024: www.washingtonpost.com/nation/interactive/2024/civil-rights-sites-alabama-selma-march/?utm_campaign=wp_post_most&utm_medium=email&utm_source=newsletter&wpisrc=nl_most&carta-url=https%3A%2F%2Fs2.washingtonpost.com%2Fcar-ln-tr%2F3e0f810%2F6676efc67a608d792c9a1e8e%2F6575da7d386724493af54680%2F9%2F43%2F6676efc67a608d792c9a1e8e.
2 A useful summary of the controversy attending J.K. Rowling's participation in the debate is given in *Glamour* magazine, 12 April

NOTES

2024: www.glamourmagazine.co.uk/article/jk-rowling-transgender-comments-controversy; see also the controversy involving Dr Kathleen Stock, formerly of Sussex University: Richard Adams, 'Sussex Professor Resigns after Transgender Rights Row', *Guardian*, 28 October 2021: www.theguardian.com/world/2021/oct/28/sussex-professor-kathleen-stock-resigns-after-transgender-rights-row.

3 See the account by Noor el-Terk, 'Remembering Tahrir Square, 10 Years on', *Al Jazeera*, 26 January 2021: www.aljazeera.com/features/2021/1/25/remembering-tahrir-square-10-years-on.

4 As a consequence of having lived in, and written about, China, I engaged for a decade in helping Chinese dissidents seeking asylum in the UK as chairman of the organisation June Fourth, and presenting evidence at the UN Human Rights Council in Geneva on the Chinese regime's human rights violations. In my view the Tiananmen Square demonstrations, and the actions taken by the Chinese authorities against them, were a major inspiration for the demonstrations in Poland, East Germany, Czechoslovakia and Romania that year, and the reason that the regimes in those countries did not attempt (except half-heartedly and briefly in Romania) to oppose them by force. Instead they crumbled; a remarkable phenomenon was seeing Erich Honecker of East Germany exposed as a Wizard of Oz figure, a naked pretender behind a screen of cardboard.

5 The remarks in this section are based on my *Democracy and its Crisis* (Oneworld, 2017) and *The Good State*.

6 James Madison, 'No. 10', *The Federalist Papers* (1787): https://avalon.law.yale.edu/18th_century/fed10.asp.

7 Richard Wike, 'Europeans Hold More Liberal Views on Moral Issues', *Pew Research Center*, 16 April 2014: www.pewresearch.org/short-reads/2014/04/16/europeans-hold-more-liberal-views-on-moral-issues/.
8 Pavlos Eleftheriadis, 'The Moral Distinctiveness of the European Union', *International Journal of Constitutional Law*, Vol. 9, No. 304 (2011): https://academic.oup.com/icon/article/9/3-4/695/657628.
9 Grayling, *Good State*.

8 Roads to *Pax Humana*

1 Grayling, *For the Good of the World*. To repeat the declaration of interest: I admire the courage and vigour of organisations like Extinction Rebellion and Just Stop Oil, whose earnestness is fully justified by the seriousness of what they combat. The reaction of those inconvenienced by traffic delays or horrified by artworks or monuments being splashed with powder paint is wholly out of proportion to what they should feel about, for example, littoral cities being flooded, island communities drowned, droughts and devastating extreme weather events, bush and forest fires, and hundreds of millions of starving climate refugees moving across the planet in search of succour.
2 See Miranda Fricker and Katharine Jenkins, 'Epistemic Injustice, Ignorance, and Trans Experiences', in Alison Stone, Ann Garry, and Serene J. Khader (eds), *The Routledge Companion to Feminist Philosophy* (Routledge, 2017).
3 The term '*convivencia*' was coined by Américo Castro, the Spanish philologist. The claim that the Iberian Peninsula saw peaceful

coexistence between the eighth and fifteenth centuries has been vigorously challenged, some arguing that the appearance of peace was maintained by the forceful suppression of minorities. Others argue that it is a myth created in criticism of Christian persecution of Jews in various parts of medieval and post-medieval Europe. See e.g. Maria Rosa Menocal, *Ornament of the World* (Little, Brown, 2003); Dario Fernandez-Morera, *The Myth of the Andalusian Paradise* (Intercollegiate Studies Institute, 2016).

4 For some remarks on the idea that morality is a matter of good manners, unintuitive as this might at first seem, see A.C. Grayling, *What Is Good?* (Orion, 2003).

5 Grayling, *Good State*.

6 Mill, *On Liberty*. The *locus classicus* is chapter 3.

7 The full and unequivocal application of human rights in the world at large solves problems well beyond what is at stake in the 'woke wars'. These latter are fought in parts of the world where a sufficient degree of progress has been made to allow focus upon them; a cynic might say that they are 'first world problems', which would be deeply unfair to the very real injustices that discrimination causes, but the fact that they can be and are being combatted is itself a hopeful matter. There are places and situations in the world where such a focus is not at present even a possibility. Among the barriers to moving whole societies to a point where a chance for remedying injustices of these kinds can materialise is conflict, especially armed conflict, within and between states. Appealing for *convivencia* at this larger scale is what we (Nobel Peace laureates Jody Williams, Mohamed ElBaradei, Leymah Gbowee and Denis Mukwege, with sculptress Anilore Banon who created the 'Les Braves' memorial on Omaha Beach, Sundeep Waslekar of

Strategic Foresight Group, and I) did in presenting the 2019 Normandy World Peace Forum Manifesto (available to read here: https://normandiepourlapaix.fr/en/manifeste-pour-la-paix). The endeavour to achieve social justice has to happen at all scales, from the global to the individual. Because human rights are individual rights, it is at the scale of lived human experience that the fruits of the endeavour are felt when its aims are achieved. Thus it is that from the global to the individual, it is an endeavour from which none of us can stand aside.

INDEX

Page numbers preceded by n. refer to the notes section.

ableism 164
Aboriginal Australians 23–5, 63, 138, 222
abortion 27, 46, 47–50
Adams, Scott 127
Adorno, Theodor 2
adultery 40, 41, 42, 58, 120
affirmative action 99, 136–7, 139, 155
Africa 32, 135, 154
African Americans 104, 134, 150, 153
   economic progress of 167–71
   racism towards 127, 128, 138–9
   reparations for 155
   see also civil rights movement
ageism 160, 164
Albigensian Crusade 79–80
Amalekites 112

Ambedkar, Bhimrao Ramji 101–3
antisemitism 97, 128
apartheid 62, 173, 212
appropriation 69–70
Aristotle 27
Aristotle's Principle 27, 124, 203, 213, 225
Armenian people 17, 77
Arnaud Amaury 79–80
Asia 134, 156
assault 58, 59–61
atheism 151
Australia 23–5, 63, 138, 222
Austrian people 146

Bannon, Steve 75
Bantu people 138
Beauvoir, Simone de 165
belief (concept) 81, 151–3, 157

257

INDEX

Benedict VIII, Pope 85
Bentham, Jeremy 140–1
Berlin Wall 62
Bernstein, Richard 176–7
Béziers, France 79–80, 87
Bible, the 18, 82, 111, 115
   as basis for law 37–9, 45, 121
   Judah and Tamar 124–6
bin Laden, Osama 19–21, 214
Black Lives Matter 139, 162, 172, 213
Black War 23
Bosnia 97
Brexit 157
Brookings Institute 167, 169, 170
Bruno, Giordano 86
Buddhism 101
Burma 62
Bush, George H. W. 178–9
Butler, Judith 165

Calvin, John 111–12, 114, 115–18
cancelling 13–16, 213–14
   contemporary aims 19, 52–3
   definition 64
   historical examples 16–17, 52
      groups 76, 85–7, 104–5
         caste system 97–104
         Catharism 77–84
         in Chinese Cultural Revolution 89–97, 204
      individuals 127–9
         Prynne, Hester 120, 122–3, 124
         Servetus, Michael 110–19
         Tamar 125–6
         Wilde, Oscar 16, 106–10, n. 232
   justifiable examples 73–4
   marginal examples 74
capitalism 65–7, 89, 96, 183
Caribbean Community (CARICOM) 155–6
caste system 97–104
Castro, Américo n. 254
Catharism 77–84
Catholicism 39–40, 62, 78, 83, 116
CCPCC (Chinese Communist Party Central Committee) 90–5
celebrities 30
censorship 15, 71, 202
China 62, 120, 147, 174, 182–4
   Cultural Revolution 89–97, 204
   economy 67, n. 236
   human rights in 156, n 228
Christianity 18, 29, 51, 151
   Catholicism 39–40, 62, 78, 83, 116
   doctrine 80–1, 83, 85, 113–14, 118–19, 120–1
   and sin 37–41
   Protestantism 39–40, 62, 87–8
   see also Calvin, John

INDEX

see also Bible, the
civil liberties 140
  see also freedoms; rights (concept)
civil rights movement 11, 12, 139, 168
  conservative criticism of 47, 174–5, 181
class 58–9, 63, 90–1, 150, 182, 195–9
  caste system 97–104
  poverty 150, 156, 168, 183
  wealth 42–3, 142, 155, 170
climate change 12, 179–80, 212–13
Cold War 173
colonisation 32, 134, 149, 173
communism 12, 90, 183–5, 192, 204
  Marxism 172, 174, 178, 181–6, 196
  Maoism 182
community (concept) 138–9, 150
compensation 55, 58, 155
  reparations 139, 153–7, n. 245-6
compromise 195, 217–18
conscience, judgements of 42–3
conservatism 29, 46, 71, 172, 174–6, 205
  criticism of activism by 176–9, 181–2, 187
convivencia 84, 98, 216–17, 221, 225
corporations 127–8, 159, 214

Covid-19 n. 226
crime 86, 106, 120
  hate 73, 151, 152, 160
  punishment for 20, 36–7, 53–61
  and sin 36–7, 38–9, 40–1
Critical Race Theory (CRT) 70, 172, 179, 184–7, 205, 221–2
Cuba 184
culture wars, *see* wokism
Czechoslovakia 204

Dalits 99–103
Dawkins, Richard 151
de Waal, Frans n. 243-4
death penalty 42, 45, 46, 49, 56
DEI (diversity, equity and inclusion) policies 181, 184, 205, 222
Democratic Party 71
democratic systems 64–5, 199, 205–10, 219
Devlin, Patrick Devlin, Baron 44–6
Dilbert comic strip 127
disabilities 11, 63, 160, 164, 198
diversity 31, 216, 218–19
  DEI policies 181, 184, 205, 222
Douglas, Alfred 'Bosie', Lord 107–10
Dove (company) 127–8
D'Souza, Dinesh 178

Economic Policy Institute (EPI) 168–9
Egypt 193

INDEX

Ellmann, Richard 106–7
Enlightenment, the 17, 86
equality 43, 68, 136, 185–6, 200
equity 185–6
   DEI policies 181, 184, 205, 222
Erasmus 112, 114, 119
ethics 48–9, n. 228
   see also morality
Ethiopian people 137–8
ethnicity (term) 134, 160
Europe 65, 134, 154, 164, 208, 211
European Union (EU) 207
exclusion, social 36, 61, 62–4
   see also cancelling
excommunication 79, 87
expression, freedom of 15, 17, 28, 70, 200, 202–3, 224–5
   denial of 158, 201, 213–15
Extinction Rebellion 179
extremism 17–18, 179, 188
   terrorism 19–20, 88
   see also left-wing politics; right-wing politics

Fabianism 28
factionalism 96, 206
fairness 11, 14, 43, 136, 141, 210
   see also equality
famine 89
Fascism 17, n. 250
   Nazism 41, 52, 104, 146, 183
feminism 11, 12, 52, 70, 165–7

conservative criticism of 47, 175, 181
First World War 145
Floyd, George 25–6, 139
forced labour 156
   slavery 41, 56, 58, 138, 181, 195
Fox (company) 70, 178
France 77–84, 109, 117, 173
   Revolution 140, 182, 193
freedoms 17
   denial of 158, 201, 213–15
   of expression 15, 28, 70, 200, 202–3, 224–5
   of speech 178, 181, 200
   of thought 12, 176–7, 178
   see also human rights

Galileo Galilei 87
Gandhi, Mahatma 102–3
gender politics 29, 52, 70, 199
   transgenderism 162, 164–5, 191, 208, 212–13, n. 233
   see also identity politics; women
Genghis Khan 88, 183
genocide 77, 98
Georgia 146
government systems 64–5, 199, 205–10, 219
Grayling, A.C. 32–4
Great Britain *see* United Kingdom (UK)

INDEX

Greece, ancient 21–2, 50, 140, 141, 209
groups (concept) 130–4, 138–9, 145, 150–2, 220–1
gun ownership 27

Hamburg, Germany 88
Harris, Cheryl 186
Hart, H.L.A. 44, 45–6, 48, 50
hate crime 73, 151, 152, 160
Havel, Václav 204
Hawthorne, Nathaniel, *The Scarlet Letter* 120, 122–4
Heineken (company) 127–8
heresy 36–7, 50–2, 84, 85–7, 111–12
Heritage Foundation 176
Hinduism 101, 102–3
Hitchens, Christopher 151, n. 229
Hitler, Adolf 128, n. 250
Holocaust, the 25–6, 76, 77
Holodomor, the 17
homosexuality 44–8, 60, 106, 121
　homophobia 178, 195
　Wilde, Oscar 16, 106–10, n. 232
human rights 6, 48, 72, 140–5, 148–9, 160
　definition 139–40, 223–5
　and the rule of law 20–1, 22
　UN declaration on 48, 130, 140, 142–3, 152
Hume, David 26, 140
Hutu people 17, 98

identity (concept) 130, 132, 138–9
identity politics 69–70, 160, 222–3
inclusivity 12, 210
　DEI policies 181, 184, 205, 222
India 97–103, 120, 147
individuals (concept) 62–4, 130–4, 138–9, 158, 216, 220–1
influencers 30–1, 194
Innocent III, Pope 79, 80, 84, 85–6
Inquisition, the 41, 78, 114, 116, 117
institutions 64–5, 181, 189–90, 214
interests (concept) 130, 157, 217–18
　self-interests 26, 196, 219–20
　vs. rights 122, 139, 145, 158–9, 190, 199, 223–4
International Labour Organization (ILO) 156
Iranian people 145
Iraqi people 145
Islam 51, 84, 112–13, 151, 154
Israel 62, 133

Japan 120
Jennings, Ivor 146
Jews 84, 98, 103, 112–13, 132–3
　Nazi treatment of 17, 41, 52, 62, 104

INDEX

see also Judaism
Jiang Qing 96
Jim Crow laws 138, 153, 212
Jodhka, Surinder Singh 98, 100–1, 103
Johnson, Boris 30
Judah 125–6
Judaism 37–9, 51, 82, 84, 97
   see also Jews
judgement 42–4, 138
Juneteenth National Independence Day 139
Just Stop Oil 179

Kant, Immanuel n. 231
Kendi, Ibram X. 186
Kierkegaard, Soren n. 231
King Jr., Martin Luther 171, 172, 204
Knight, David M. 40–1
Ku Klux Klan 104–5
Kulak people 89
Kurdish people 145

La Croix 40–1
Lake, Cleo 155
Launceston Advertiser 23
Lauterpacht, Hersch 10
leadership 2, 30, 204
Lebin Yan 89
left-wing politics 27–8, 73, 174–6, 191–3
   attitudes to cancel activism 71, 181
   author's personal views 33
   socialism 66–7, 173

Leicester, Simon de Montfort, Earl of 80
LGBTQ+ rights 29, 190, 211, 212
   lesbianism n. 233
   transgenderism 162, 164–5, 191, 208, 212–13, n. 233
   see also homosexuality; sexual orientation
liberal (term) 64, 67
Liberalism 65–8, 71, 175–6, 192
libertarianism 67, 158, 177, 192
life, right to 142, 143–4
Lutherism 88, 112

McCarthy, Joseph 174–5
McIntosh, Peggy 69, 222
McWhorter, John 70
Madison, James 206
Magdeburg, Germany 87–8
Maher, Bill 70
male influencers 30–1
Malik, Nesrine 171–2
Mandela, Nelson 204
Mao Zedong 89–97, 182, 183
marriage 27, 29, 70, 120, 156, n. 233
Marx, Karl 182–3, 184
Marxism 172, 174, 178, 181–6, 196
masculinity 30–1
Me Too movement 70, 121, 162, 213
media 29–30, 172, 176–7
   social media 29, 74
   influencers 30–1, 194

INDEX

role in cancel activism 12–13, 14, 123, 214–15
Melians 22
men 30–1, 121–2, 136, 165–7
Mexico 62
Mill, John Stuart 45, 219
moderates 28, 73, 181, 192–3, 205
see also Liberalism
Moldova 146
Montfort, Simon de 80
morality 41–2, 56, 120–1, 218, n. 228
and the law 42–3, 45–6, 48, 50
Mubarak, Hosni 193
murder 21, 55, 57–8, 60, 76
Myanmar 97, 133

National Institute of Health (NIH) 134
nations (term) 146, 147, 224
Native Americans 222, n. 236-7
Navayana 101
Nazism 41, 52, 104, 146, 183
Neoliberalism 67–8
Netherlands, the 112
New York magazine 176
New York Times 176
Newsweek 176
Nietzsche, Friedrich 22
9/11 attacks 19–20, 151, n. 229
North Korea 149, n. 236
Northern Ireland 62
Nuremberg Laws 41
Nussbaum, Martha n. 230

obligations (concept) 130–1, 132
offence (emotion) 159–61
Organisation of Islamic Cooperation (OIC) n. 228
Orwell, George 177
othering 36, 61–4
see also cancelling

Palestine 62, 115
Paley, William 87
pandemics 158, n. 226
Pappenheim, Graf Gottfried Heinrich zu 87
Parker, James 23–4
party politics 206–10
see also left-wing politics; right-wing politics
PC (political correctness) 12, 47, 164, 173, 176–9
people (term) 146–7, 148–9
People's Liberation Army (PLA) 90, 94–6
Peter of Vaux-de-Cernay 80
Peters, Edward 78
Pew Research Center 70, 71, 208
Philip II, King of France 79, 83–4
Plato 115, 209
pluralism 46, 50
Poland 204
political correctness (PC) 12, 47, 164, 173, 176–9
political views 152
moderates 28, 73, 181, 192–3, 205

INDEX

see also left-wing politics; right-wing politics
positionality 31–4
positive discrimination 135–8
postmodernism 68, 172–3, 174
poverty 150, 156, 168, 183, 195–9
prejudices 150, 205, 206, 219–21
principles 21, 22–3
privacy 47, 48–9
Prohibition 41, 57
ProQuest 177
prostitution 120, 124–5
Protestantism 39–40, 62, 87–8
    Calvin, John 111–12, 114, 115–18
Prynne, Hester 120, 122–3, 124
punishment 20, 36–7, 53–61
Puritanism 120, 124

Queensberry, John Douglas, Marquess of 108–9

race (term) 134–5, 160, n. 238
racism 11, 32, 134, 195, 208, 212
    corporate examples 127–8
    historical examples 29, 103, 127
        segregation 104, 138
        slavery 41, 56, 58, 138, 181, 195
        see also civil rights movement; Jews
    inequality in US 167–73

    and positive discrimination 137–8
    see also caste system
rape 58–9, 60, 76, n. 241
Raymond VI, Count of Toulouse 79
Reformation, the 39, 86, 117
rehabilitation 55, 60
religion 27, 123, 216
    as basis of law 44, 49
    criticism and defence of 152–3
    heresy 36–7, 50–2, 84, 85–7, 111–12
    inclusion in hate speech laws 151, 160
    persecution of groups 77–85, 87–8
    and sin 37–41
    see also belief (concept)
relocation policies 23
Renaissance 114, 117
Renmin Ribao (RMRB) 92, 93
reparations 139, 153–7, n. 245–6
Republican Party 27, 71
retribution 54–5
revolutions 89–97, 140, 182, 185, 193
Richelieu, Cardinal n. 230-1
rights (concept) 130–4, 139, 190, 217–18
    conflicts of 158–61, 199, 223–4
    see also freedoms; human rights

INDEX

right-wing politics 27–9, 103, 191–3
   criticism of activism 70–3, 176–9, 181–2, 187, 200
   conservatism 29, 46, 71, 172, 174–6, 205
RMRB (*Renmin Ribao*) 92, 93
Rohingya people 62, 133
Roma people 63
Rome, ancient 56, 58–9, 78, 120, 140, 183
Rufo, Christopher 172
Russia 89, 146, 182, 193, 204
   see also Soviet Union
Rwanda 98

Samarkand, Uzbekistan 88
same-sex marriage 29, 70
Second World War 88, 173, n. 229
   Holocaust, the 25–6, 76, 77
   Nazism 41, 52, 104, 146, 183
segregation 104, 138
self-interests 26, 196, 219–20
September 11 attacks 19–20, 151, n. 229
Servetus, Michael 110–19
sex (biology) 138, 160, 165
sexism 11, 69, 195, 212
sexual intercourse 31, 45, 58–9, 82–3, 120–4, n. 233
   prostitution 120, 124–5
sexual orientation 15, 70, 160, 164–5, 199, 208
   homophobia 178, 195

homosexuality 44–8, 60, 106, 121
lesbianism n. 233
LGBTQ+ rights 29, 190, 211, 212
sin 36–42
slavery 41, 56, 58, 138, 181, 195
   reparations 153–6
'smaller state' policies 27
social exclusion 36, 61, 62–4
   see also cancelling
social justice movements 68, 74–5, 180, 205, 224
social media 29, 74
   influencers 30–1, 194
   role in cancel activism 12–13, 14, 123, 214–15
socialism 66–7, 173
South Africa 32, 104, 173
Soviet Union (USSR) 12, 149, 174, 182–4, n. 236
   see also Russia
Spain 84, 112, 114, 216
Spanish Inquisition 41, 78
speech, freedom of 178, 181, 200
   see also expression, freedom of
Sri Lanka 149
Stalinism 89, 182
Stoicism 140, 141
student activism 90–6, 175
Sumerians 120

Tamar 125–6
taxation 27, 43, 66–7, 195, 199
terrorism 19–20, 88

INDEX

Thatcher, Margaret 67
theft 57–8
theocracies 44
Thernstrom, Stephan 177
Thomas, Bartholomew Boyle 23–4
Thomas Aquinas 86, 113
thought, freedom of 12, 176–7, 178
Thucydides 21
Tibetan people 145
Time magazine 176
Torquemada, Tomas de 78, 112
TransAfrica n. 246
transgenderism 162, 164–5, 191, 208, 212–13, n. 233
Trump, Donald 29, 30, 47, 205, n. 236, n. 243
Turkish people 17, 120, 145
Tutsi people 17, 77, 98

Uighur people 145
Ukraine 89, 146
United Arab Emirates (UAE) 156
United Kingdom (UK) 43–4, 140, 144, 145, 151
   colonialism 98–9
   connections with slavery 153–4, 155
   decriminalisation of homosexuality 44–6
   political systems 27, 173, 205–6
United Nations (UN) 103, 165–6, 173

human rights declaration 48, 130, 140, 142–3, 152
United States of America (USA) 14, 59, 62, 140, 173–4, 212
   abortion 47–50
   Constitution 47–8, 140, 186
   equality in 43–4, 165
   official racial categories 134–5
   and Osama bin Laden 19–21, 214
   political divisions within 27, 29, 174, 192
   political system 66, 205–6
   race politics in 138–9, 167–73, 204
   and slavery 41, 153–4
USSR (Soviet Union) 12, 149, 174, 182–4, n. 236
see also Russia

Vanini, Cesare Guilio 86
Vietnam War 173

Wałęsa, Lech 204
Wall Street Journal 176
war 20–1, 76, 88, 158, 202
wealth 42–3, 142, 155, 170, 195–9
Weinstein, Harvey 72
West, Kanye 128
Western societies 11, 29, 57–8, 72, 181
Wilde, Oscar 16, 106–10, n. 232
wokism 70, 162–3, 164, 172, 210, 213–15

definition of 'woke' 72, 180
radical activism 181, 184, 189–91, 200–1, 205, 214
right-wing hostility towards 28, 29, 47
Wolfenden Report 44, 46
women 121–6, 136, 208, 222
abortion 27, 46, 47–50

feminism 11, 12, 52, 70, 165–7
conservative criticism of 47, 175, 181
Wright Austin, Sharon 170–1

Zoroastrianism 51

A. C. Grayling is the Founder and Principal of the New College of the Humanities at Northeastern University, London, and its Professor of Philosophy. Among his many books are *The God Argument*, *Democracy and Its Crisis*, *The History of Philosophy*, *The Good State* and *The Frontiers of Knowledge*. He has been a regular contributor to *The Times*, *Guardian*, *Financial Times*, *Independent on Sunday*, *Economist*, *New Statesman*, *Prospect* and *New European*. He appears frequently on radio and TV, including *Newsnight* and *CNN News*. He lives in London.

ALSO BY A. C. GRAYLING

Who Owns the Moon?: In Defence of Humanity's Common Interests in Space

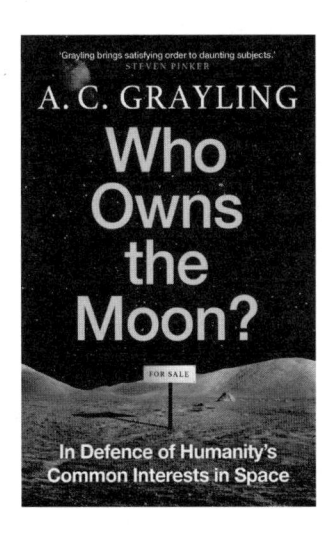

As the world's superpowers and corporations jostle for control in space, A. C. Grayling asks: who *really* owns our planet?

Silicon for microchips; manganese for batteries; titanium for missiles. The moon contains a wealth of natural resources. So, as the Earth's supplies have begun to dwindle, it is no surprise that the world's superpowers and wealthiest corporations have turned their eyes to the stars. As this new Space Race begins, A. C. Grayling asks: who, if anyone, owns the moon?

From feudal common land to the vast, nationless expanse of Antarctica, Grayling explores the history of the places which no one, and therefore everyone, owns. Examining the many ways this so-called *terra nullius* has fallen victim to 'the tragedy of the commons' – the tendency for communal resources to be exploited by a few at the expense of the many – *Who Owns the Moon?* puts forward a compelling argument for a bold new global consensus, one which recognises and defends the rights of everyone who lives on this planet.

COMING AUTUMN 2025

For The People: Fighting Authoritarianism, Saving Democracy

By A. C. Grayling

Around the world the foundations of democracy, freedom, civil liberties are being eroded – what can be done?

Are we living through the end of the democratic moment? While democracy once seemed the bedrock of Western societies, the past few decades have revealed a fragile reality. Once liberal countries are turning to authoritarianism, wealthy individuals and corporations are interfering with elections evermore flagrantly, and faith in democracy has plummeted among every demographic. What went wrong?

From gerrymandering and partisanship to corporate interference and tainted donations, A. C. Grayling reveals the forces undermining our democratic ideals and offers bold solutions. An urgent wake-up call to the risks this poses to us all, *For The People* reminds us why democracy remains worth fighting for.